The Real Holy Grail

Other books published by the Orthodox Research Institute include:

Saint Cyril of Alexandria. *Against Those Who Are Unwilling to Confess that the Holy Virgin Is Theotokos*. Introduction, Greek Text and English Translation by Protopresbyter George Dion. Dragas

Rev. Dr. Steven Bigham. *Early Christian Attitudes toward Images*

Panagiotes K. Chrestou. *Greek Orthodox Patrology: An Introduction to the Study of the Church Fathers*. Edited and translated by Protopresbyter George Dion. Dragas

Protopresbyter George Dion. Dragas. *Ecclesiasticus I: Introducing Eastern Orthodoxy*

Protopresbyter George Dion. Dragas. *Ecclesiasticus II: Orthodox Icons, Saints, Feasts and Prayer*

Protopresbyter George Dion. Dragas. *The Lord's Prayer according to Saint Makarios of Corinth*

Protopresbyter George Dion. Dragas. *On the Priesthood and the Holy Eucharist: According to St. Symeon of Thessalonica, Patriarch Kallinikos of Constantinople and St. Mark Eugenikos of Ephesus*

Protopresbyter George Dion. Dragas. *Saint Athanasius of Alexandria: Original Research and New Perspectives*

Protopresbyter George Dion. Dragas. *St. Cyril of Alexandria's Teaching on the Priesthood*

Alphone and Rachel Goettmann. *The Spiritual Wisdom and Practices of Early Christianity*

Protopresbyter John S. Romanides. *An Outline of Orthodox Patristic Dogmatics*, in Greek and English. Edited and translated by Protopresbyter George Dion. Dragas

The Real Holy Grail

An Orthodox Response to Dan Brown's Deceptions in Angels and Demons and The Da Vinci Code

Metropolitan Bishoy

General Secretary of the Holy Synod of the Coptic Orthodox Christian Church; Metropolitan of Damiette, Kafr el-Sheikh, and Barrary, Egypt; and Abbot of the Monastery of Saint Demiana for Nuns, Egypt

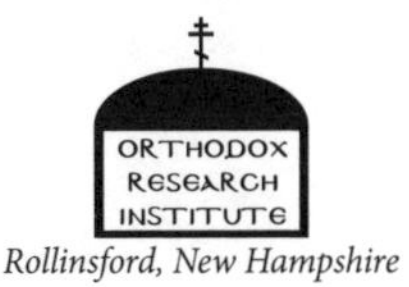

Rollinsford, New Hampshire

Published by Orthodox Research Institute
20 Silver Lane
Rollinsford, NH 03869
www.orthodoxresearchinstitute.org

Library of Congress Control Number: 2007921545

ISBN-13: 978-1-933275-14-7
ISBN-10: 1-933275-14-6

For His Holiness Pope Shenouda III,
in deep gratitude for courageously standing up for the Truth
and upholding the true Orthodox Christian faith

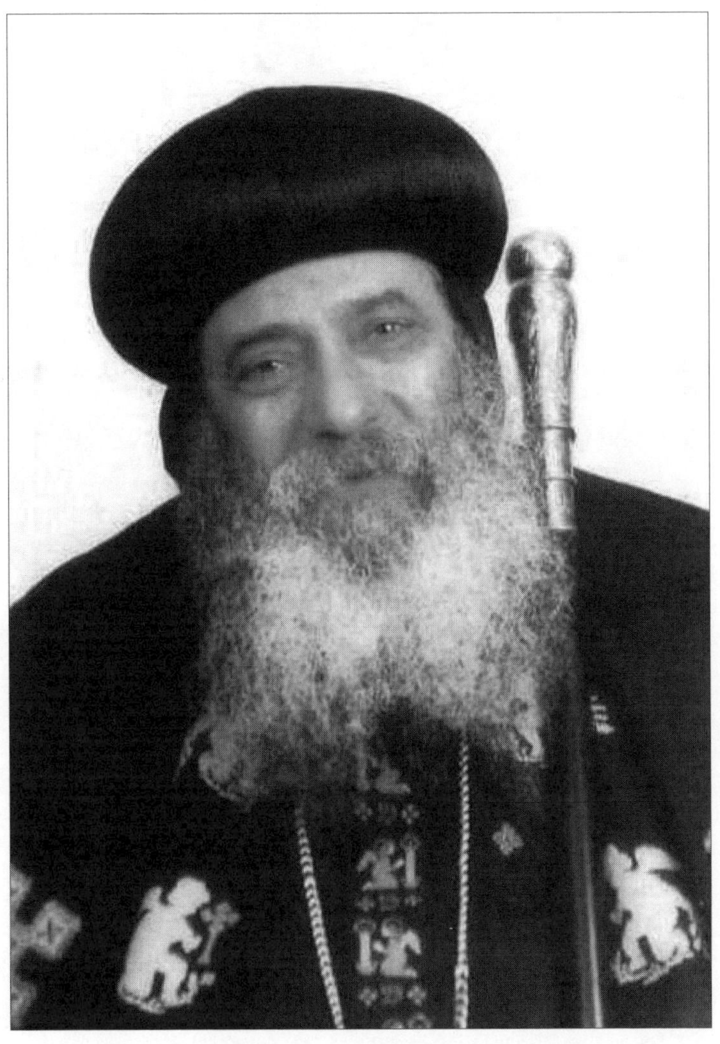

HIS HOLINESS POPE SHENOUDA III

117th Pope of Alexandria and Patriarch of the See of Saint Mark

Contents

FACT:

Not neglecting the prophecy written
by Moses in the Book of Genesis:

Dan shall be a serpent by the way,
A viper by the path,
That bites the horse's heels
So that its rider shall fall backward.
I have waited for Your salvation,
O LORD!
(Genesis 49:17)

Dan Brown's outlandish claims
in *The Da Vinci Code* and
Angels and Demons about
the Divinity of Jesus Christ,
Mary Magdalene, Christianity,
the Gospels, the goddess,
and the Christian Church
are entirely false.

All descriptions in defense of the
Almighty God the Father, His
Only-Begotten Son — our Lord God
and Savior Jesus Christ, His Holy Bible,
and His Holy universal and apostolic
Church in this apologetic work
are accurate.

The Coptic Orthodox Church is a
member of the Oriental family of
Orthodox Churches which includes:
the Syrian Orthodox Church of Antioch
and all the East, the Armenian Orthodox
Catholicosate of Etchmiadzin, the Armenian
Orthodox Catholicosate of Cilicia,
the Malankara Orthodox Syrian Church,
the Ethiopian Orthodox Church, and the
Eritrean Orthodox Church.

INTRODUCTION

Woe to those who call evil good, and good evil;
Who put darkness for light, and light for darkness.

Isaiah 5:20–21

Angels and Demons and *The Da Vinci Code*, by author Dan Brown, although classified as works of "fiction," are really not what they herald themselves to be. By blurring the lines which separate truth from fiction, they have deceived many with a plethora of lies about God and Christianity.

In *Angels and Demons*, the reader is constantly presented with differing views about the existence of God and Who He really is. Throughout, we see God defined in a number of ways: He is referred to as science, as an enormous source of energy, as Gaea—the pagan goddess of the earth, as The Force, as Buddha, as Mother Earth, as the singularity, and as Yahweh.[1] We are also told that "pure energy is the father of creation,"[2] instead of God Himself. *Angels and Demons* claims that science, rather than the Church, can provide the answers to all man's questions about the universe, and is the means by which man can understand God. In addition, Dan Brown launches a serious assault on the Roman Catholic Church, accusing it of manipulating the truth and murdering those whose views threatened her own, or those who threatened to expose so-called truths which she was trying to conceal. Referring to Brown's idea of science versus religion, the *New York Times* points out:

> With *Angels and Demons* ... the book finds the enormously likable Langdon pondering antimatter, the big-bang theory, the cult of the Illuminati and a threat to the Vatican ... Yet this is merely a warm-up for the mind-boggling trickery that *The Da Vinci Code* has in

[1] Brown, *Angels and Demons*, 72, 110, 174, 484.
[2] Ibid., 72.

> store … As in his *Angels and Demons*, this author is drawn to the place where empirical evidence and religious faith collide. And he creates a bracing exploration of this realm …[3]

In *The Da Vinci Code*, among many other false claims, Dan Brown tells us that Jesus Christ was a mortal prophet; that He was married to Mary Magdalene and that they had a child; that Constantine promoted Jesus to a deity at the Council of Nicaea, and that Constantine "commissioned and financed a new Bible, which omitted those gospels that spoke of Christ's human traits and embellished those gospels that made Him godlike."[4] Again, we are told that the Roman Catholic Church used fear and violence to conceal the true facts about Christianity, and also that the Church was responsible for the demise of the sacred feminine. In addition, Dan Brown asserts his desire to promote the glorification of the feminine goddess through secret and sacred sex rituals such as the *hieros gamos*, and advocates the worship of Venus — the Roman goddess of love. We are also told that man can only come to know God through sexual union with woman outside of the context of Christian marriage, and that woman is god because through childbirth she is the giver of life.

With this information in mind, we must ask: Is it accurate to call all of this fiction? No, quite obviously it is not.

It is theology.

It is Christology.

It is heresy.

It is the rewriting of history.

It is lies masquerading as truth.

It is a redefinition of Christianity.

It is a call for a return to paganism.

It is a new religion …

But what Dan Brown is describing in *Angels and Demons* and *The Da Vinci Code* can most certainly not be categorized as fiction. What Brown

---

[3] Maslin, "Spinning a Thriller from the Louvre."

[4] Brown, *The Da Vinci Code*, 254.

is actually doing, is presenting all of these elements under the guise of fiction, while at the same time, claiming that they are factual. But even Brown's "facts," which he maintains are historically informed, are full of inaccuracies and historical discrepancies.

It is worth mentioning that Dan Brown is the author of two earlier novels titled *Digital Fortress* and *Deception Point*. While these novels do not attack Christianity, they do represent sexual immorality, and contain much sexual innuendo, and profanity. Dan Brown is also working on his next novel—*The Solomon Key*—which will explore the secret society of the Freemasons, and which, it is speculated, will be published in 2007. However, these books are not the aim of my discussion. But my focus here is to present, from a Coptic Orthodox perspective, biblical, theological, and Christological truths in response to the major false claims made in *Angels and Demons* and *The Da Vinci Code* against the Lord Jesus Christ, His Church, and His Holy Bible. My emphasis, however, will be on *The Da Vinci Code*; because after all, it is this novel specifically which threatens the faith of Christians. Along the way, I will also very briefly highlight the central errors Dan Brown has made with regard to the art, architecture, and the secret societies mentioned in this very same novel.

In both *Angels and Demons* and *The Da Vinci Code*, Dan Brown attacks the Roman Catholic Church exclusively; but while the Coptic Orthodox Church does not necessarily agree with all of the Catholic Church's dogmas, we do not approve of the lies being propagated against the Catholic Church. It is also important to be aware that in attacking the Roman Catholic Church, Brown has, at the same time, ridiculed the Christian faith of millions. All Christians, including the Orthodox, the Anglicans, and the Protestants—not just Catholics—hold as true the fundamental belief in one God and find utterly objectionable the suggestion that God has a female counterpart; they profess that Jesus Christ is His Only-Begotten Son Who was incarnate in the fullness of time, and that He was never married; and they have no doubts whatsoever concerning the authenticity of the Gospels and the Holy Bible in its entirety. It is, therefore, unacceptable for Dan Brown to casually come along and discredit a faith embraced by so many; Christians have every right to be angered by Dan Brown's violent attack on their faith. Interestingly, more than one scholar has further commented that if "such lies and errors had been directed at the Koran or the holocaust they would have justly provoked a world uprising."[5] But what most people have completely overlooked, or rather have not noticed, is the fact that *The Da Vinci Code*, does not only slight Christianity as whole, but it does indirectly and subtly attack the major patriarchal religions of the world. Yes, even Judaism and Islam are demeaned. Having sold fifty million hardback copies and being translated into forty-four languages since it was first published in 2003, *The Da Vinci Code* in particular, has become a worldwide cultural phenomenon. But Christianity stands firm and unshaken: "The best protection against Satan's lies is to know God's truth."[6]

The Fall of Satan

> The great dragon was cast out, that serpent of old, called the Devil and Satan, who deceives the whole world; he was cast to the earth, and his angels were cast out with him.
> How you are fallen from heaven, O Lucifer, son of the morning! How you are cut down to the ground, you who weakened the nations![7]

The pride and consequent fall of Satan, although occurring before the creation of man, is arguably the most unfortunate event in the history of all creation. At the very beginning of the world, the Devil was the first one to perish; and when he saw man made in the image and likeness of God, he broke forth into a fit of anger and malevolent jealousy. It was a fit of envy that did not end. Satan's profound resentment towards humanity fills his entire being; it is a dreadful fire that has not ceased to rage deep within him; it is a hatred that not only continues unwaver-

---

[5] Roman Catholic Archbishop, Rev. Angelo Amato, quoted in Reuters, "Boycott 'Da Vinci Code' Film: Top Vatican Official."

[6] Anonymous.

[7] Rev. 12:9; Isa. 14:12.

ingly, but grows stronger with every passing minute. The Wicked One and the Enemy of God is determined to bring down every last human being. He has sworn to turn the entire race of humankind away from God's love, God's law and God's Truth. Satan's ultimate goal is to see all of humanity deny the only true God—the Father of our Lord, God and Savior Jesus Christ. He causes man to follow other gods, and through every possible means, he seeks to prevent man from inheriting eternal salvation. Saint John Chrysostom says that, "the whole essence and effort of the Devil is to separate and remove our attention from God..."[8] Saint Cyprian also explains:

> ...the Apostle Peter, in his epistle, forewarns and teaches, saying, "Be sober, and watch; because your adversary the Devil as a roaring lion, goes about seeking anyone to devour." He goes about every one of us; and even as an enemy besieging those who are shut up (in a city), he examines the walls, and tries whether there is any part of the walls less firm and less trustworthy, by entrance through which he may penetrate to the inside. He presents to the eyes seductive forms and easy pleasures, that he might destroy chastity by the sight. He tempts the ears with harmonious music, that by the hearing of sweet sounds, he may relax and enervate Christian vigor. He provokes the tongue by reproaches... he promises earthly honors, that he may deprive of heavenly ones; he makes a show of false things, that he may steal away the true; and when he cannot hiddenly deceive, he threatens plainly and openly, holding forth the fear of turbulent persecution to vanquish God's servants. [He is] always restless, and always hostile, crafty in peace, and fierce in persecution.[9]

For Satan, there is no greater satisfaction than to see a soul perish, and throughout history, he has employed various methods of attack in order to annihilate man. Persecution was one of his earliest primary weapons. Tertullian—a scholar in early Christianity—tells us that "Persecution seems to proceed from the devil, by whom the injustice which constitutes persecution is perpetrated... we believe that persecu-

---

[8] www.copticmail.com.

[9] Saint Cyprian, *Treatise X: On Jealousy and Envy*, *ANF*, 5.491.

tion comes to pass, no question, by the devil's agency."[10] In Matthew 10:16–25, Jesus warns His followers to expect persecution; and in Mark 10:39, He also says that the blood of Christians would be shed for His name. During most periods of persecution, Christians were ordered to abandon their belief in Christ and offer sacrifices to pagan idols. If they refused, they were usually imprisoned and suffered the most excruciating tortures, followed by the most violent of deaths. Scriptures were confiscated, churches burned or demolished, clerics abused, and Christian civil servants deprived of their citizenship. Off and on, for two and a half centuries following AD 64, Christians suffered suspicion, attacks, and official repression.[11] But for Christians, death meant victory. Satan's evil plan failed, and Christianity flourished.

However, when violence through persecution did not weaken Christianity, heretics spurred on by Satan, introduced heresies in order to dissuade the world from following God. Instead of violence, Satan used heresy in an attempt to sway humanity with beliefs and doctrines that contradicted or undermined the apostolic faith; often through the misuse of Scripture. Although heresies existed prior to, and at the time of persecution, it was not until later that the most treacherous heretics emerged. These heretics were, in fact, so dangerous, that the Church was required to convene ecumenical councils to adjudicate the charges of heresy raised against them. The pages of history give numerous accounts of such men whose heresies were eradicated by the Church, albeit with great anguish and difficulty. The most controversial heresies were those of Arius and Nestorius,[12] but they were rejected at the Councils

[10] Tertullian, *De Fuga In Persecutione, ANF*, 4.117.

[11] Walford, *Encyclopedia of the Early Church*, vol. 2, 673.

[12] In brief, Arius' heretical teachings denied the Divinity of Christ and were summed up in the phrase, "There was a time when He [the Son] was not." The problem with Arius' heresy was that he taught that God the Father existed for time without God the Son which, in turn meant, that 1) the Son was created by the Father, and 2) the Son was not consubstantial (of the same essence) with the Father. Arius' teachings were refuted by the Church at the Council of Nicaea and the refutation of this heresy was articulated by Saint Athanasius the Apostolic in his treatise, *On the Incarnation*. Nestorius taught that there are two persons in Christ: a divine person—the

of Nicaea (325) and Ephesus (431) respectively. Heresy was an effective weapon against the Church because it denied Orthodox doctrine. In turn, a denial of Orthodox doctrine led to a denial of Scripture, while a denial of Scripture led to unbelief. And, of course, without faith in Jesus Christ as the true God, incarnate for humankind's salvation, no person could be saved. This is precisely what Satan strove to achieve; but with the condemnation of hundreds of heresies across the ages, he was once again defeated.

But Satan, that most stubborn foe of ours, never gives his malice a rest. Indeed, he is most ruthless when he feels that man is freed from his clutches.[13] So now, he has waged the most savage war against the Church since the ascension of the Lord Jesus Christ. This is a war unlike any other. It is a war without physical violence. It is a war entirely free of the sword, but already the casualties are numbered in the millions. Satan has deceived many by unleashing his most dangerous weapons to date: The novels of Dan Brown. In this book, we shall try to respond to this satanic war.

Metropolitan Bishoy
October, 2006 AD

Logos, dwelling in a human person—the man Jesus. He also said that the blessed Virgin Saint Mary could not be called the Theotokos—Mother of God.

[13] Tertullian, *On Repentance*, *ANF*, 3.662.

CHAPTER ONE

What is Dan Brown's Agenda?

Christ is still sold, but not any more for 30 coins,
but to publishers and booksellers for billions of coins.

Raniero Cantalamessa[1]

Surprisingly, Dan Brown professes to be Christian. When asked, "Are you a Christian?" in an interview featured on his official website, he offers the following reply:

> Yes. Interestingly, if you ask three people what it means to be Christian, you will get three different answers. Some feel being baptized is sufficient. Others feel you must accept the Bible as absolute historical fact. Still others require a belief that all those who do not accept Christ as their personal savior are doomed to hell. Faith is a continuum, and we each fall on that line where we may. By attempting to rigidly classify ethereal concepts like faith, we end up debating semantics to the point where we entirely miss the obvious — that is, that we are all trying to decipher life's big mysteries, and we're each following our own paths of enlightenment. I consider myself a student of many religions. The more I learn, the more questions I have. For me, the spiritual quest will be a lifelong work in progress.[2]

In other words, Dan Brown is not Christian. After all, his novels are grounded in fraudulent assertions, and his response seems to be just another lie in his continuing spree of dishonesty. Further, two of his books — *Angels and Demons* and *The Da Vinci Code* — are so blatantly anti-Christian, that we are hard-pressed to believe that a Christian

---

[1] Roman Catholic Rev. Raniero Cantalamessa in his Good Friday homily before Roman Catholic Pope Benedict XVI in St. Peter's Basilica, quoted in D'Emilio, "Opus Dei Asks for 'Da Vinci' Disclaimer."

[2] Accessed at http://www.danbrown.com/novels/davinci_code/faqs.html, on 3 August, 2006.

could have authored them. No true Christian would even entertain the notion of writing material of such a blasphemous and heretical nature. It is important to note that Brown flatly denies that *The Da Vinci Code* is anti-Christian saying that, "This book is not anti-anything."[3] In another interview he states: "I worked very, very hard to make the book fair to all parties. Yes, it's explosive. I think there will be people for whom this book will be — well, 'offensive,' may be too strong a word. But it will probably raise some eyebrows."[4] Brown's *The Da Vinci Code* has not only 'raised eyebrows,' but it has enraged the entire Christian world. Archbishop Reverend Angelo Amato, the number two official in the Vatican doctrinal office, called the book "stridently anti-Christian ... Full of calumnies, offences and historical and theological errors regarding Jesus, the gospels and the Church."[5]

But to be less harsh on Brown, he genuinely appears to lack a clear understanding of what it means to be Christian in the true sense of the word; and his 'yes' and 'no' response to the question regarding his Christianity points to the fact that he does not even seem to know what he actually believes. Brown appears to be content with calling himself Christian, so long as he is a Christian by his own rules, and on his own terms. But suppose we accepted Dan Brown's claim to being Christian as the truth? It would not then be unreasonable to liken him to Judas Iscariot who betrayed Jesus Christ. If Dan Brown is, in reality, Christian, we could say that Judas Iscariot's betrayal of Christ, in comparison with Brown's, is quite tame.

Either way, it is apparent that Satan himself has employed Dan Brown as his pawn in his quest to destroy Christianity. And this, exactly, is Brown's purpose. *Angels and Demons*, and especially *The Da Vinci Code*, were written with two specific goals in mind: firstly, to obliterate the Church and Christianity; and secondly, to supplant Christianity by a new pagan religion which embraces the worship and glorification of

---

[3] http://www.danbrown.com/novels/davinci_code/faqs.html.

[4] Brown, quoted in Morris, "Explosive New Thriller Explores Secrets of the Church."

[5] Amato, quoted in "Boycott 'Da Vinci Code' Film: Top Vatican Official.

a goddess or goddesses through complete sexual permissiveness. Steve Kellmeyer observes:

> Why is *The Da Vinci Code* popular? Because he's written an earlier book *Angels and Demons* which has essentially the same plot, essentially the same anti-Christian slams within it, but it's not nearly so popular as this book; the major difference is how he treats sexuality. This book is centered around it... He says that sex is holy... and that women are to be treated like goddesses, that is, like... God. In this society... women, who are eighty percent of the book-buying market, see these messages in Dan Brown's novel and say, "I don't care if the rest of it is wrong, this much is right.[6]

Brown reconfirms his personal belief in the "sacred feminine," implying that under the dual sovereignty of pagan gods and goddesses the world was a better place:

> Two thousand years ago, we lived in a world of Gods and Goddesses. Today, we live in a world solely of Gods. Women in most cultures have been stripped of their spiritual power. The novel [*The Da Vinci Code*] touches on questions of how and why this shift occurred... and on what lessons we might learn from it regarding our future.[7]

More precisely, Dan Brown's purpose is: to deny the Divinity of Christ; discredit the true Gospels; distort and rewrite the history of Christianity; reintroduce Gnosticism and radical feminism; propagate pagan Ancient Egyptian and Graeco-Roman (or civilo-pagan) theology, as well as neo-pagan and pantheistic theology; and call the world to return to pagan beliefs. In both *Angels and Demons* and *The Da Vinci Code*, he endorses a new religion where people can believe whatever they please and where the worship of Mother Nature is one the chief principles. By promulgating this purpose in his writing, Brown falsely confirms for atheists and pagans that pagan beliefs are a part of the original, truest, and more superior religion; while for Christians, he creates anxieties

---

[6] Steve Kellmeyer (Author: *Fact and Fiction in The Da Vinci Code*), interview in *The Da Vinci Code Deception* DVD.

[7] http://www.danbrown.com/novels/davinci_code/faqs.html.

and calls into question the foundation of their faith. What is also evident is Brown's endorsement of the elimination of all seemingly patriarchal religions. In his opinion, any religion which worships a single male god is a gender-biased, sexist, oppressing religion.

Dan Brown sets out to achieve his aims through an endless web of deceptions, falsehoods, and invented history. In *Angels and Demons* we are presented with a "FACT" page and an Author's Note stating: "References to all works of art, tombs, tunnels, and architecture in Rome are entirely factual… The brotherhood of the Illuminati is also factual."[8] But in an interview, Brown tells us that, "Separating Illuminati fact from fiction can be difficult on account of the massive quantities of misinformation that has been generated about the brotherhood."[9] Dan Brown attacks the Roman Catholic Church, accusing the Vatican of ruthlessly hunting the Illuminati. But if according to Brown, identifying Illuminati fact is so difficult, how then can we possibly take any of his information about the Illuminati and the Catholic Church seriously?

In *The Da Vinci Code* there are also explicit claims of fact. The first page of the novel reads: "FACT… All descriptions of artwork, architecture, documents, and secret rituals in this novel are accurate."[10] Dan Brown has no training in history or in theology, but he repeatedly makes dubious claims that all of his novels are meticulously researched. Yet even Brown's first novel, *Digital Fortress*, earned scorn for its erroneous depiction of cryptography and its overly negative depiction of Spain.[11] In interviews with Brown, he has made the following comments: "One of the aspects that I try very hard to incorporate in my books is that of learning… When you finish the book [*The Da Vinci Code*]—like it or not—you've learned a ton. I had to do an enormous amount of re-

[8] Brown, *Angels and Demons*. The Illuminati are an alleged secret society and enemies of the Roman Catholic Church in *Angels and Demons*.

[9] Accessed at http://www.danbrown.com/novels/angels_demons/interview.html on 3 August, 2006.

[10] Brown, *The Da Vinci Code*.

[11] Shea and Sri, *The Da Vinci Deception*, 12.

search ..."[12] And also: "One of the many qualities that make *The Da Vinci Code* unique is the factual nature of the story. All the history, artwork, ancient documents, and secret rituals in the novel are accurate ..."[13] The problem with all of these statements, however, is the fact that most of the so-called "facts" in Brown's books are *not* fact! Dan Brown's mockery of the truth and his anti-Christian/pro-pagan agenda have not gone unnoticed by Christian and historical scholars. One of the most accurate assessments of Brown's objectives is articulated by Tom Allen when he says:

> Brown knows exactly what he is doing. He has a deep hostility to the Christian Gospel and to the Catholic Church in particular and fills his novel not merely with mistakes but with malicious lies with one end in view: to attack the Gospel of Jesus Christ and replace it with a resurgent pagan mythos. Along the way, he smears Catholics as mass murderers, and tells bald-faced lies about the Council of Nicaea, the origins of the Bible, and Jesus' supposed "transformation" into God at the hands of the early Church. He sets out a blizzard of phony "facts" about history, art, religion, theology ... He intimidates with fake erudition, gets even easily verifiable facts embarrassingly wrong, claims to celebrate the "sacred feminine" ... and, to be brief, tells rank lies under the guise of writing "fiction" for one main purpose: to fix in the reader's mind the conviction that "everything our fathers taught us about Christ is *false*."[14]

Carl Olson in his article in *Envoy* magazine echoes a similar viewpoint saying that Dan Brown intends for his readers to accept the following:

> ... humanity needs to abandon its silly belief that Jesus is Savior and God, and get back to worshipping the "sacred feminine," especially as personified by Jesus' (supposed) wife, Mary Magdalene. Also important to Brown: the Catholic Church needs a woman's

---

[12] Brown, quoted in Morris, "Explosive New Thriller Explores Secrets of the Church."

[13] Brown, quoted in Mariampolski, "Secrets Hidden in Plain View: Dan Brown Delivers the Most Exciting Novel of the Season."

[14] Shea and Sri, *The Da Vinci Deception*, 2–3.

> touch (Mary Magdalene again; not Mary the Mother of God) and must abandon her obsession with doctrine, orthodoxy, and truth. Finally, religion is stupid and for simpletons; all we need is, well, the "sacred feminine."[15]

In other words, Dan Brown objects to people adhering to any particular organized religion. Instead, he advocates that each individual should adhere to any combination of beliefs, ideals, values, and practices which he or she personally sees fit, provided that the beliefs, ideals, values, and practices encompass the exaltation of women and the worship of any female pagan goddess or goddesses—preferably though, Venus. The goddess Venus is mentioned many times throughout Brown's work, and it is quite clear that she is much adored by him.

Of course, not everyone agrees that *Angels and Demons* and *The Da Vinci Code* are bad. Literally hundreds of comments, articles, discussions, television programs, and documentaries are singing the praises of Dan Brown, hailing him as a genius. But the general consensus by those who are aware of the false claims contained in Brown's novels, is that *Angels and Demons* and *The Da Vinci Code* are extremely dangerous books. Why are they so very dangerous? Because "most people know very little about the historical origins of Christianity, so they are easy targets for a cleverly packaged, sensationalized set of lies;" and also because they offer an attractive relativistic attitude toward truth and religion, a dislike for religious authority, and a belief that reality is malleable and can be customized to each person's wishes."[16] In the coming chapters, I will examine Dan Brown's motives outlined in the points above, and highlight just how harmful his ideas are. But before we move on, I would like to comment on *The Da Vinci Code* motion picture and make a comparison with the book itself.

---

[15] Olson, "Cracking Up The Da Vinci Code: Bad writing. Bad history. Bad theology. Did I Mention it Was Bad?"

[16] Niederauer, "How Dark the Con of Man: Some Responses to *The Da Vinci Code* (The Novel and Soon the Film)."

CHAPTER TWO

The Da Vinci Code Motion Picture

How can a film contain so many clues yet remain utterly clueless?

Michael Phillips (Chicago Tribune)[1]

On May 16, 2006, Columbia Pictures' *The Da Vinci Code*[2] was previewed by Sony Pictures making its debut at the opening of the 59th Cannes Film Festival and in New York simultaneously. The film was directed by Ron Howard, and it is interesting to note that Dan Brown himself is one of the film's executive producers. Part of Sony's 'grand' marketing plan was to shroud *The Da Vinci Code* in complete secrecy until the last minute. It was kept so secret, in fact, that before its release, it did not first undergo a test or media screening or even a special screening for critics. In the movie industry, this practice is quite rare; and is usually undertaken only by studios who know that their film is a failure, in the hope of avoiding attention from critics. With reference to *The Da Vinci Code*, Sony claims that the motion picture was kept secret in order to give it an air of excitement and mystery. Valerie Van Galder, president of domestic marketing for Sony Pictures said, "There was an inordinate amount of interest in this film, and we wanted to contain the excitement and anticipation ... We wanted people to see the movie for themselves and not react to months of endless debate about the movie."[3] When speaking about the topic of test screenings on CNN in 1998, *Da Vinci Code* director Ron

[1] Phillips, "Movie Review: The Da Vinci Code."

[2] *The Da Vinci Code*, a Columbia Pictures (Sony) release. Director Ron Howard. Screenplay Akiva Goldsman, based on the novel by Dan Brown. Producers Brian Grazer, John Calley. Director of photography Salvatore Totino. Editors Dan Hanley, Mike Hill. Includes disturbing images, violence, some nudity, some profanities, brief drug references and sexual content. Running time: 2 hours, 32 minutes.

[3] Waxman, "Da Vinci Code: The Mystery of the Missing Screenings."

Howard stated: "What I would hate to do is put the movie out there, find out that the audience is confused about something or upset about something that you could have fixed, and go, 'I had no idea they'd respond that way.'"[4] So it is rather surprising that he agreed to forgo a test screening for *The Da Vinci Code*—a decision that he has most likely regretted.

Ironically, Howard's choice of words those many years ago, best describe the reaction of most critics to *The Da Vinci Code* motion picture: the majority were indeed "confused" or "upset." They were so unimpressed by the film and gave it such poor reviews, that many certainly believe it was kept under wraps in order to give critics little time to write their reviews, providing minimal time for the public to read them before the premiere. The *New York Times* confirms that "journalists first saw the movie on Tuesday night, barely allowing them time to write their articles for the Wednesday premiere and Friday opening in theaters around the world."[5] Roman Catholic Reverend Thomas J. Euteneuer comments on this method of secrecy saying: "Ted Baehr of *MovieGuide* has pointed out that Sony is so nervous about this risky *Da Vinci* venture that they issued it with little time for a backlash. 'Big movie studios dump movies worldwide without previews because they are afraid that the word-of-mouth will kill them. They are trying to get as much money as quickly as possible before the public finds out they have a stinker.'"[6] And it is no wonder Sony was nervous. *The Da Vinci Code* immensely disappointed the Cannes crowd. Here are just a few examples of the predominantly negative reviews:

> A preview of the $US125 million film billed as a "thrilling murder investigation that unearths the biggest cover-up in human history" has been greeted by disappointed whistles and snickers from some 2,000 journalists. (ABC)[7]

> Critics largely panned the cinematic version … The movie did receive some lukewarm praise, but the majority of the response was

[4] Ibid.
[5] Waxman, "Da Vinci Code: The Mystery of the Missing Screenings."
[6] Euteneuer, "The Da Vinci Mess-Final Edition: Leonardo's Revenge."
[7] AFP, "Stars Shrug Off 'Da Vinci Code' Reviews."

> highly critical … One scene during the film, meant to be serious, elicited prolonged laughter from the audience. There was no applause when the credits rolled; instead, a few catcalls and hisses broke the silence. (CNN)[8]
>
> Hanks … seems to sleepwalk through the part… Yet when he delivers the film's dead-serious climactic line — "You're the last living descendant of Jesus Christ" — it got a derisory laugh from the Cannes crowd. (TIME)[9]
>
> Shrugs of indifference, some jeering laughter and a few derisive jabs … The Cannes audience clearly grew restless as the movie dragged on to two and a half hours and spun a long sequence of anticlimactic revelations … Some people walked out during the movie's closing minutes…and there was none of the scattered applause even bad movies sometimes receive at Cannes. (AP)[10]

On May 19th, *The Da Vinci Code* officially opened around the world, screening in 3,735 cinemas in the US alone. But despite having already received disparaging reviews, it earned an estimated $224 million worldwide in its first three days. The sole reason for *The Da Vinci Code's* success in its first week, was the eagerness of fans to see the novel which they held in such high regard on the big screen. Quite simply, there was a great degree of curiosity to see how closely the plot and screenplay adheres to the book: Would the film be just as gripping? Would it correctly depict all of the scenes? Would it be as readers had pictured it? The answers are no, no, and no. From an artistic and cinematic viewpoint, *The Da Vinci Code* was criticized primarily because:

It is too long:

> "Sitting through this overlong, overbaked, overbearing anti-thriller felt like watching a team of academics solve cryptograms for two and a half hours straight." (HOUSTON CHRONICLE)[11]

---

[8] http://davincireview.com/reviews.html.
[9] Corliss, "The Da Vinci Code Mystery Revealed!"
[10] http://davincireview.com/reviews.html.
[11] Biancolli, "It's Just Like the Book, Without Any of the Interesting Parts."

> It's preposterous, overlong, and saddled with a sloppy denouement that defines the term "anti-climax." ... the production as a whole is a lumbering mess ... *The Da Vinci Code* (the movie) is a mediocre thriller, with too few thrills and too much predictable action ... The prosaic story does not warrant the film's epic length. Two-and-one-half hour movies are supposed to be something special. This one is merely overlong. (REELVIEWS)[12]

> "Director Ron Howard relentlessly patronises his audience with ... flashbacks to The World of Ancient History, and the whole thing goes on for hours and hours." (BBC)[13]

> "A 'Da Vinci Code' That Takes Longer to Watch Than Read." (NEW YORK TIMES)[14]

It is too crammed:

> "... a movie both overstuffed and underwhelming ... The movie is so anxious about covering as much of the novel's ground as possible that it never gives the actors any breathing space." (NEWSWEEK)[15]

> "Then there are more codes. There are so many, in fact, it's like that "I Love Lucy" episode in which the chocolates rumbled down the conveyor belt too fast to box them all." (NEW YORK DAILY NEWS)[16]

It contains too many flashbacks, making it too confusing:

> "Attempting to use flashbacks to put the religious puzzle together, the film loses the book's urgency and page-turning mystery." (CHICAGO TRIBUNE — Matt Pais)

> The explanatory flashbacks are horrible and, instead of reading the book at your own pace, plowing through all the twists, double twists and triple twists, leads you to ask of the movie, "Why is ev-

[12] Berardinelli, "The Da Vinci Code."
[13] Arendt, "The Da Vinci Code (2006)."
[14] Scott, "A 'Da Vinci Code' That Takes Longer to Watch Than Read."
[15] Ansen, "A Disappointing 'Da Vinci Code.'"
[16] Bernard, "It Didn't Work For Me: Howard's 'Da Vinci' is Paint-By-Numbers."

eryone pretending to be someone else?" One missed clue and the whole mystery would be lost forever. (FILMS IN REVIEW.COM)[17]

The movie does, however, take a while to accelerate, popping the clutch and leaving rubber on the road as it tries to establish who is who, what they're doing and why... Along the way the film pauses... to flash back, in desaturated color, to traumatic events in the childhoods of various characters (Langdon falls down a well; Sophie's parents are killed in a car accident; Silas stabs his abusive father)... There are also glances further back into history, to Constantine's conversion, to the suppression of the Knights Templar and to that time in London when people walked around wearing powdered wigs. Through it all Mr. Hanks and Ms. Tautou stand around looking puzzled. (NEW YORK TIMES)[18]

Periodically, Howard speeds us off to crowded, computer-generated visions of ancient Rome or the Holy Land or Ye Olde England for whirlwind history lessons that whip by so speedily you can barely take in the information, but not fast enough so that you don't notice how tacky they look. Then there are the desaturated-color flashbacks to traumatic moments in our characters' histories: little Robert falling down a well, the car crash that kills Sophie's parents or the back story of Silas, the albino hit man with a penchant for self-flagellation. Anyone who hasn't read the book will find this latter utterly confounding, as will anyone who has. (NEWSWEEK)[19]

Anyone who hasn't read Brown's novel will probably be confused about the convoluted historical conspiracy, and anyone who has will be equally bored, since Goldsman and Howard add nothing new to Brown's plot. All they manage to do is highlight the book's weaknesses, making the film neither a worthy adaptation nor a successful stand-alone product. (LAS VEGAS WEEKLY)[20]

Worst, "The Da Vinci Code" goes in for a flash flood's worth of flashbacks, whether to illustrate the brutality of various Christian

[17] Alexander, "The Da Vinci Code."

[18] Scott, "A 'Da Vinci Code' That Takes Longer to Watch Than Read."

[19] Ansen, "A Disappointing 'Da Vinci Code.'"

[20] Bell, "The Da Vinci Code."

> wars, or to show Langdon falling down a well as a child, or Sophie and her mysterious grandfather. It's like a flashback fire sale. (CHICAGO TRIBUNE — Michael Phillips)[21]

The same *Chicago Tribune* article further complains of the movie's soundtrack,

> "And early on, when one character turns to another and says, "You're in grave danger," you think, well, everyone's in grave danger of being burned alive by Hans Zimmer's overheated score."[22]

as does *USA Today*:

> "Perhaps the movie's most grating element is its overheated and intrusive score by Hans Zimmer."[23]

And so, it is apparent just how dreary and baffling the film has turned out be. I first viewed *The Da Vinci Code* with a small group of people from my diocese who have not read the book. Thereupon, they all mentioned that *The Da Vinci Code* motion picture is exceptionally difficult to follow, and that many of the scenes and flashbacks are unintelligible. I would tend to agree with them, seeing that to fully understand the movie, one must first understand the book. I say this not to encourage the reading of *The Da Vinci Code* or to endorse the watching of the film — I advise against both because of their detrimental effect on the Christian spiritual life — but merely to point out the danger of the film. Although the movie is a much "watered-down" version of the book, it is as dangerous, since anyone who has not first read *The Da Vinci Code*, will be motivated to read it in order to comprehend the film.

But now to turn our attention to the film's purpose. *The Da Vinci Code* novel and *The Da Vinci Code* motion picture share the same primary purpose: that is, as I have mentioned, to raise doubts about cornerstone aspects of the Christian faith and to uproot Christianity. As in the novel, the film tells the audience that the Catholic Church

[21] Phillips, "Movie Review: The Da Vinci Code."

[22] Ibid.

[23] Puig, "For 'Da Vinci' Suspense, Read the Book."

is responsible for "the greatest cover-up in human history;" namely, concealing the fact that Christ was married to Mary Magdalene and fathered a daughter, whose bloodline has survived into present-day Europe. *The Da Vinci Code's* royal historian and supposed theological expert Leigh Teabing, states that it is a secret so great, that "if revealed, it would devastate the very foundations of Christianity." Fortunately for Christianity, the film considerably tones down or omits the book's more controversial elements; so much so, that critics have noted Christianity has nothing to worry about. Christianity's very foundations have not been "devastated," and actually, they have not even been shaken. Reviewers also have stated that the film is so obviously unbelievable that the average person should easily recognize it as fantasy. The *New Yorker's* Anthony Lane states unequivocally:

> The Catholic Church has nothing to fear from this film. It is not just tripe. It is self-evident, spirit-lowering tripe that could not conceivably cause a single member of the flock to turn aside from the faith. Meanwhile, art historians can sleep easy once more, while fans of the book, which has finally been exposed for the pompous fraud that it is, will be shaken from their trance.[24]

MSNBC's David Ansen says:

> "The Roman Catholic Church can rest easy … This film is not likely to topple Christianity as we know it."[25]

Lastly, and along the same lines, *Reelviews* and the ABC respectively affirm:

> … a better title for *The Da Vinci Code* might be *Much Ado about Nothing*. When you boil away the hype and hysteria, all that remains is a pedestrian murder mystery that isn't sufficiently challenging or scandalous to raise anyone's hackles … The story is so outlandish as to be obviously fabricated, with a minimal basis in fact. *The Da Vinci Code* is fanciful enough that it requires no debunking — that much should be obvious to anyone attending the film.[26]

[24] Lane, "Heaven Can Wait: The Da Vinci Code."
[25] Ansen, "A Disappointing 'Da Vinci Code.'"
[26] Berardinelli, "The Da Vinci Code."

> Dismissing the much-hyped Hollywood production as morally corrupt, clergymen have condemned the movie as a vile mixture of outright fiction, half-truths and volatile spiritual matters. But one senior church official heaved a sigh of relief after catching the preview saying the movie was so unbelievable it posed no threat to their faith.[27]

The Da Vinci Code film makes essentially the same preposterous anti-Catholic and anti-Christian statements as those in Dan Brown's bestseller, including the following:[28]

- [The Knights Templar] were butchered by the Catholic Church.
- By the 1300's the Templars had grown too powerful, too threatening, so the Vatican issued secret orders to be opened simultaneously all across Europe. The pope had declared the Templars Satan worshippers and said God had charged him with cleansing the earth of these 'heretics.' The plan went off like clockwork. The Templars were all but exterminated. [It] was October 13th, 1307—a Friday.
- [Mary Magdalene was] smeared by the Church in 591 Anno Domini, poor dear. Mary Magdalene was Jesus' wife."
- Women then are a huge threat to the Church. The Catholic Inquisition soon publishes what may be the most blood-soaked book in human history... *Malleus Maleficarum—The Witches' Hammer*... It's instructing the clergy on how to locate, torture, and kill all free-thinking women... In three centuries of witch hunts, 50,000 women are captured; burned alive at the stake.
- For two-thousand years, the Church has rained oppression and atrocity upon mankind. Crushed passion and ideal alike, all in the name of their walking God. Proof of Jesus' mortality can bring an end to all that suffering; drive this church of lies to its knees... Jesus must be shown for what He was: not miraculous, simply man. The dark con can be exposed. Mankind can finally be set free...

[27] AFP, "Stars Shrug Off 'Da Vinci Code' Reviews."

[28] The following quotes in this section are direct quotations taken from *The Da Vinci Code*, a Columbia Pictures (Sony) release.

As in the novel, it similarly makes false claims about the Divinity of Jesus Christ and the Emperor Constantine, saying:[29]

- [Until a vote at the Council of Nicaea in 325] … Jesus was viewed by many of His followers as a mighty prophet and a great and powerful *man*, but a man nevertheless — a *mortal* man.
- The Good Book did not arrive by facsimile from heaven. The Bible as we know it was finally presided over by one man — the pagan emperor Constantine.
- Constantine may have been a life-long pagan but he was also a pragmatist. And in 325 Anno Domini he decided to unify Rome under a single religion: Christianity … Christianity was on the rise; he didn't want his empire torn apart … And to strengthen this new Christian tradition, Constantine held a famous ecumenical gathering known as the Council of Nicaea. And at this council, the many sects of Christianity debated and voted on everything from the acceptance and rejection of specific gospels, to the date of Easter, to the ministering of the sacraments, and of course, the mortality of Jesus.
- [The Gospel of Phillip] … was rejected at the Council of Nicaea, along with any other gospels that made Jesus appear human and not divine.

And finally, it repeats the same lies about Mary Magdalene and Leonardo's *The Last Supper*, which are contained in the book:[30]

- And now let me show you the Grail. I trust you recognize *The Last Supper* — the great fresco by Leonardo da Vinci … The chalice resembles a cup, or vessel, or more importantly, the shape of a woman's womb. Now the Grail has never been a cup. It is quite literally this ancient symbol of womanhood. And this case a woman who carried a secret so powerful that if revealed it would devastate the

[29] Ibid.
[30] Ibid.

very foundations of Christianity... Now then, what about the figure on the right hand of our Lord seated in the place of honour? Flowing red hair, folded feminine hands, hint of a bosom... My dear, that's Mary Magdalene... Notice how Jesus and Mary are clothed? Mirror images of each other... And venturing into the even more bizarre, notice how Jesus and Mary appear to be joined at the hip and are leaning away from each other as if to create a shape in the negative space between them. Leonardo gives us the chalice.

- Now, listen to this; it's from the Gospel according to Phillip... "And the companion of the Saviour was Mary Magdalene. Christ loved her more than all the disciples. And used to kiss her on the..."
- And this is from the Gospel of Mary Magdalene herself... "And Peter said, 'Did He prefer her to us?' And Levi answered, 'Peter, I see you contending against the woman like an adversary. If the Saviour made her worthy, who are you indeed to reject her?'" And then my dear, Jesus goes on to tell Mary Magdalene that it's up to her to continue His Church. Mary Magdalene, not Peter. The Church was supposed to be carried on by a woman. Do you realise that Mary was descended from kings just as her husband was. Now my dear, the word in French for Holy Grail... Sang Real it means 'royal blood...'
- When the legend speaks of the chalice that held the blood of Christ, it speaks, in fact, of the female womb that carried Jesus' royal bloodline... Mary was pregnant at the time of the crucifixion. For her own safety and for that of Christ's unborn child, she fled the Holy Land and came to France. And here it is said she gave birth to a daughter—Sarah.
- Imagine then... that Christ's throne might live on in a female child. You asked what would be worth killing for. Witness the greatest cover-up in human history. This is the secret the Priory of Sion has defended for over twenty centuries. They are the guardians of the royal bloodline; keepers of the proof of our true past. They are the protector of the living descendents of Jesus Christ and Mary Magdalene.
- Mary Magdalene lived out her days in hiding. And the zealots pursued her still; even in death; trying to destroy proof of her exis-

tence. But she always had her knights — brave men sworn to defend her. You see to worship before her sarcophagus; to kneel before the bones of Mary Magdalene, was to remember all those who were robbed of their power; who were oppressed. Ultimately, the Priory hid her remains and the proof of her bloodline until most believed her sarcophagus — the Holy Grail — was finally lost in time.

The movie's emphasis is on these ideas together with a recurring sympathy for, and adulation of Mary Magdalene; unlike the book which focuses on the same, but has a very strong preoccupation with a broader notion of the sacred feminine and the worship of the goddess. Both the book and the film do, however, present Mary Magdalene as the *lost sacred feminine*, although this is not explicitly stated in the film. In the following chapters, we will examine these claims, but the similarities notwithstanding, the film does deviate from the book in a number of areas. Before the release of *The Da Vinci Code*, director Ron Howard indicated in an interview that he would ensure the movie is faithful to the book saying, "It would be ludicrous to take on this subject and then try to take the edges off. We're doing this movie because we like the book."[31] But the "edges" are exactly what Ron Howard did take off. *USA Today* tells us that "Though [the film] retains most of the complex twists and turns of Dan Brown's best seller, some of the elements that have sparked protests among Christians — questions about the divinity of Jesus Christ and his lineage — have had their edges smoothed."[32] One such element is the belief in the sacred feminine and the goddess. As I have previously pointed out, one of chief goals of Dan Brown's work is to bring the world back to the worship of the goddess, and to venerate her through the sexual union of man and woman. The book is laden with neo-pagan and sexual concepts; the film, on the other hand, makes only one exact reference to Mother Nature, the goddess, and the sacred feminine when Leigh Teabing says: "Constantine was Rome's supreme

[31] Ron Howard, quoted in Byron Barlowe, "Da Vinci Code: The Movie."
[32] Puig, "For 'Da Vinci' Suspense, Read the Book."

holy man… his people had worshipped a balance between nature's male deities and the goddess, or sacred feminine." There is also only one reference to the worship of the goddess though sexual union when the *The Da Vinci Code's* protagonist, Harvard Symbologist[33] Robert Langdon says: "The pagans found transcendence through the joining of male and female." To which heroine Sophie Neveu replies, "People found God through sex?" Langdon then responds saying: "In paganism, women were worshipped as route to heaven, but the modern Church has a monopoly on that, in salvation through Jesus Christ."[34] All of this is quite astonishing seeing that the film is supposed to be a very close adaptation of "a novel drawing so heavily on the sacred feminine…"[35]

Another central element of the book that is noticeably and deliberately avoided by the film is the hieros gamos pagan sacred sex ritual, which we will discuss in Chapter Eight of this book. Despite its being at the core of the book's theology, it is significantly downsized in the movie. In the book, Brown provides a five-page explanation of hieros gamos, including a graphic depiction of the ritual; but in the film it is featured as a few separate flashbacks, totaling no more than approximately three seconds, and devoid of any explanations. The film also omits numerous discussions and references to Venus—the Roman goddess of female sexual love—and her association with the male/female physical union; Eros—the Greek God of sexual love; Baphomet—an alleged pagan fertility god; Christianity's "stealing" of pagan symbols, rites, and holy days; ritualistic sex in Solomon's Temple; and the androgynous physical union between Yahweh and Shekinah; all of which are featured predominantly in the book.

We can only speculate as to why all of these elements were omitted from *The Da Vinci Code* movie: perhaps it is an attempt by Ron Howard to conceal the book's true, evil nature; perhaps he was afraid of the

---

[33] In reality, Harvard University has no Department of Symbology; it is an invention by Brown.

[34] These are direct quotations taken from The Da Vinci Code, a Columbia Pictures (Sony) release.

[35] Brown, The Da Vinci Code, Acknowledgements.

negative ramifications and ridicule that is likely to have resulted if they were included, or perhaps he rightly felt that incorporating such nonsense would push audiences too far. Unlike Brown, Howard it seems, knew where to draw the line, exercising discernment in steering clear of what would have added to an already highly implausible film.

The final point I would like to make about the film is that it includes additions and changes not originally incorporated into Dan Brown's book. For example, in the final scenes, we see hero Robert Langdon and Sophie Neveu entering an underground vault at Rosslyn Chapel where they discover the secret Sangreal documents, but this does not occur in the novel. In the film, there is also the Star of David imprinted on a piece of stone located on the altar of the chapel, while in the book this star is said to be imbedded in the floor of Rosslyn; but Rosslyn Chapel in reality does not contain either. There are also major changes in the plot such as Sophie's meeting with the Priory of Sion at the end of the film, and her learning that Jacques Saunière[36] was not her grandfather. The movie further includes a discussion about prayer by Robert Langdon which does not feature in the book, in which he says:

> History shows us that Jesus was an extraordinary man, a human inspiration; that's it. That's all the evidence has ever proved. But when I was a boy, when I was down in that well Teabing told you about, I thought I was going to die Sophie. But what I did… I prayed. I prayed to Jesus to keep me alive so I could see me parents again, so I could go to school again, so I could play with my dog. Sometimes I wonder if I wasn't alone down there. Why does it have to be human or divine? Maybe human is divine. Why couldn't have Jesus been a father and still be capable of all those miracles?[37]

As *USA Today* states: "Where the movie deviates from the book most strikingly is in the attitude of the lead character, Harvard symbology professor Robert Langdon… The movie tones down his academic fervor and ratchets up his spirituality. In the book, he does not discuss

---

[36] In *The Da Vinci Code*, Jacques Saunière is the curator of the Louvre Museum and the novel's first murder victim.

[37] Direct quotation from The Da Vinci Code, a Columbia Pictures (Sony) release.

prayer. In the movie, he does."[38] The film of course makes, many more minor changes but it is unnecessary to list these here. What we must further remember that the film is merely an *adaptation* of the book, so changes in the story are to be expected. However, what the film has, or has not, changed aside, *The Da Vinci Code* is a movie of which we should be wary because it makes essentially the same claims against our God and our faith in Him.

---

[38] Puig, "For 'Da Vinci' Suspense, Read the Book."

CHAPTER THREE

Brown's Sources, the Priory of Sion, and the Knights Templar

It's to his advantage to insist that the farrago of lies and misrepresentations used to prop up the conspiracy theory in The Da Vinci Code ... is part of the historical record or at least in general circulation.

Laura Miller (Salon Magazine)[1]

Dan Brown is being commended as though he has discovered some unknown "truth" about Christianity, but he is not the first to bring this, and other ridiculous claims to light. What he has done, is simply resurrected old, tired, unverified assertions that have existed for decades but have never been taken seriously because of their recognizably false nature.[2] In *Unlocking da Vinci's Code: The Full Story*—a documentary which aired on the U.S. National Geographic Channel in 1994—even Brown admitted, "That information has been out there for a long time, and there have been a lot of books about this theory. The interesting thing is that they're all history tomes that sit in the back corner of bookstores. *The Da Vinci Code* has taken a lot of that informa-

[1] Miller, "The Da Vinci Crock."

2 There have been other similar blockbusters in the last couple of decades. The Australian Barbara Thiering attained brief notoriety with her book *Jesus the Man*, based on an extraordinary supposed decoding of the Dead Sea Scrolls and showing that, once more, Jesus had been married to Mary Magdalene. Thiering adds the twist that they divorced and that Jesus married again. Nobody takes Thiering seriously except occasional radio and TV chat shows... Then there was a book called *The Tomb of God*, by Richard Andrews and Paul Schellenberger, published in 1997, proposing that the body of Jesus is buried under a hill in southern France (cf. *Seattle Pacific University Magazine*, "Decoding The Da Vinci Code: The Challenge of Historic Christianity to Post-Modern Fantasy.")

tion and put it in a different genre, and there's an enormous part of the population now that's hearing this for the first time. And it feels brand new." The *New York Daily News* declares that Dan Brown's "research is impeccable." But the "history tomes" from which Brown has gleaned his "impeccable research" are little-known, small, approximately 500-page texts that have been laughably rejected and identified as grossly inaccurate by serious academics and scholars alike.

Brown draws upon a number of such sources for his abundant lies, and he actually cites his principal sources prominently within *The Da Vinci Code* narrative (266, 273–4). These are esoteric histories, namely: *Holy Blood, Holy Grail* by Michael Baigent, Richard Leigh, and Henry Lincoln; *The Templar Revelation: Secret Guardians of the True Identity of Christ* by Lynn Picknett and Clive Prince; *The Goddess in the Gospels: Reclaiming the Sacred Feminine* and *The Woman with the Alabaster Jar: Mary Magdalen and the Holy Grail* both by Margaret Starbird; as well as *The Gnostic Gospels* by Elaine Pagels which is a work of feminist "scholarship." The information which he has unashamedly lifted from these books, includes those false claims about: the marriage between Jesus Christ and Mary Magdalene, the Priory of Sion and the Knights Templar, the true and Gnostic gospels, the Emperor Constantine, the Council of Nicaea, paganism, the origins of Christianity, the hieros gamos, and goddess worship; to name but a few. In fact, just about all of Brown's outrageous claims come from the highly non-credible works mentioned. Bluntly put, Brown has invented much of what he says, and for the rest of his claims he has relied on the absurd inventions of others.

Another author, Lewis Perdue, says that the facts in *The Da Vinci Code* are close to the fiction in his two books, *The Da Vinci Legacy and the Daughter of God*:

> When I first read *The Da Vinci Code*, it wasn't the mass of similarities that truly bothered me; but what I found were, there were mistakes that I'm the only person who made, that were replicated in the *The Da Vinci Code*. For example, when I wrote *The Da Vinci Legacy*, I made a mistake and wrote that Leonardo's *Codex Leicester* was written on parchment, but the only other place on the

> planet that appears is in Brown's *The Da Vinci Code*. And there are other things, for example, I have female spiritual characters that the heroine is related to, just as Brown does. In both *The Da Vinci Legacy* and *The Da Vinci Code*, the fourth art expert of his type is murdered; he leaves his last message written in his own blood on his own body... And there are other things: in both books, a murdered curator leaves a unique gold key to the heroine inside a wood-painted work of art which refers to a holy line. This gold key, which turns no lock, links to a Zurich bank safe deposit box containing yet another container locked by a combination and containing very important secrets. If I hadn't written *The Da Vinci Legacy* twenty years before the *The Da Vinci Code* came out, I would have thought I got all my ideas from Brown.[3]

For his part, Brown says he has never heard of Lewis Perdue, and did not have any prior knowledge of his books.[4] But the book from which Brown draws most extensively is *Holy Blood, Holy Grail*. It is a pseudo-historical work first published in 1982; "a self-described "shocking international best-seller" that most scholars ignored or found to be either amusing or insulting."[5] *Holy Blood, Holy Grail* discusses the legend of the Holy Grail, and includes stories about secret gospels, the Dead Sea Scrolls, and medieval secrets. The authors introduce the notion that the Holy Grail is not the chalice used by Jesus Christ at the Last Supper; but by falsely dividing the medieval French term "*Sangraal*" (Holy Grail), into "*sang*" (blood) and "*raal*" (royal) to create the term "royal blood," they claim that the Holy Grail is a metaphor for the royal bloodline of Jesus Christ and Mary Magdalene.[6] They attempt to prove this idea of royal blood by attesting that Jesus was of the Line of David and that Mary Magdalene was of the Tribe of Benjamin—their alleged union (the blending of two royal bloodlines), thereby creating a royal lineage.

---

[3] Lewis Perdue, interview in *The Da Vinci Code Deception* DVD.

[4] Ibid.

[5] Olson, "Cracking Up The Da Vinci Code."

[6] Margaret Starbird, on page 26 of her book, *The Woman with the Alabaster Jar: Mary Magdalen and the Holy Grail*, makes the same error. Brown, as we will see, copies this idea from both Baigent, Leigh, and Lincoln; and Starbird.

Holy Blood, Holy Grail brings together these facts centered on a secret society called the Prieurè de Sion (the Priory of Sion) — which according to Baigent et al. was founded in 1099 in Jerusalem by the crusader Godfroi de Bouillon — and their military arm the Knights Templar.

The Priory are said to have been the guardians of secret documents and other proofs that Mary Magdalene was the wife of Jesus and that she carried His child with her when she fled to what is now France after the Crucifixion, becoming, figuratively, the Holy Grail in whom Jesus' blood was preserved. According to the authors, the progeny of Jesus and Mary Magdalene intermarried with the locals, eventually founding the Merovingian dynasty of Frankish monarchs. Although they were deposed in the eighth century, the Merovingian lineage has allegedly not been lost; but the Priory has kept watch over its descendants, awaiting an auspicious moment when it will reveal the astonishing truth and return the rightful monarch to the throne of France, or perhaps even a restored Holy Roman Empire.[7] Baigent et al. further claim that the Priory boasted an illustrious list of heads or "grand masters" — such as Leonardo da Vinci, Isaac Newton, Victor Hugo, and Sandro Filipepi who is more commonly known as Botticelli — and that evidence for this was found in the *Dossiers Secrets* (Secret Dossiers) deposited in Paris' Bibliothèque Nationale in the 1960's. The *Dossiers Secrets* are also said to contain details of the Knights Templar, lists of the Templars' grand masters, and Merovingian genealogies. *Holy Blood, Holy Grail* attests that these parchments were originally discovered in 1890's in the small French town of Rennes-le-Château by a young priest named Abbé Bérenger Saunière. Also listed by the authors as a grand master of the Priory, is man by the name of Pierre Plantard de Saint-Clair whom they describe as "the direct descendent, through Dagobert II, of the Merovingian Kings" whose "descent has been proved legally by the parchments ... discovered by Abbé Saunière in his church at Rennes-le-Château ... in 1891."[8] It is from Pierre Plantard that Baigent et al. took most of their information.

---

[7] Miller, "The Last Word: The Da Vinci Con."

[8] Baigent, Leigh, and Lincoln, Holy Blood, Holy Grail, 214-15.

The majority of falsehoods which Dan Brown presents in *The Da Vinci Code* are essentially the same as those in *Holy Blood, Holy Grail*; the major difference being that Brown's false claims are presented within the context of an exciting, page-turning mystery. On a page titled "FACT" before the prologue, Brown makes the following assertion: "The Priory of Sion — a European society founded in 1099 — is a real organization. In 1975 Paris's Bibliothèque Nationale discovered parchments known as *Les Dossiers Secrets*, identifying numerous members of the Priory of Sion, including Sir Isaac Newton, Botticelli, Victor Hugo, and Leonardo da Vinci." Within the story itself, Brown refers to the *Dossiers Secrets* as the "Sangreal documents." On page 353 of *The Da Vinci Code* Brown also uses the same list of grand masters' names which appears on page 131 of *Holy Blood, Holy Grail*. He has not, however, included *Holy Blood's* claims about Abbé Saunière or Pierre Plantard de Saint-Clair, but he does borrow their names for characters in *The Da Vinci Code*: the main murder victim in Brown's novel is Jacques Saunière, while Plantard and Saint-Clair are names that Brown asserts the Merovingian families (of which heroine Sophie Neveu is a descendant) adopted in order to protect their true identity. *The Da Vinci Code's* historian Leigh Teabing, is also named after two of *Holy Blood, Holy Grail's* authors—"Leigh" is taken from "Richard Leigh," and "Teabing" is an anagram of "Baigent."

The second primary source from which Brown has obtained his "facts" is *The Templar Revelation* — another pseudo-historical work — that puts forward the same theories as *Holy Blood, Holy Grail*. Picknett and Prince discuss the Priory of Sion, the Dossiers Secrets, the list of Grand Masters, the Knights Templar, Abbé Saunière's parchments, Pierre Plantard de Saint-Clair, and a relationship between Jesus and Mary Magdalene, but with some differences in perspective. The authors of *The Templar Revelation* go even further than Brown and Baigent et al., claiming that Jesus and Mary Magdalene were unmarried sex partners in a "sacred marriage" and performed erotic pagan sex rites (such as the hieros gamos). They describe Mary Magdalene as a high priestess with whom the "king-priest" Jesus united through sexual union, in order to receive wisdom and His full divine power, so as to be acknowledged as king.[9] Moreover, Picknett and Prince introduce the Priory of Sion, not as an organization with political motivations, but as a secret cult of goddess worshippers who have preserved the secret of Christ's true mission, which, "if made public, would shake the very foundations of both the Church and State."[10] What is interesting is that while *The Templar Revelation* itself draws heavily on *Holy Blood, Holy Grail,* it criticizes some of its theories. In order to highlight just how much Dan Brown has used *Holy Blood, Holy Grail* and *The Templar Revelation,* below are other major false claims made by Brown which parallel the information in these two books:

1. Dan's Deceptions about the Priory of Sion, the Sangreal Documents, and the Royal Bloodline

- The Priory of Sion ... was founded in Jerusalem in 1099 by a French king named Godefroi de Bouillon, immediately after he had conquered the city (*DVC,* 171).[11]
- King Godefroi was allegedly the possessor of a powerful secret—a secret that had been in his family since the time of Christ. Fearing his secret might be lost when he died, he founded a secret brotherhood—the Priory of Sion—and charged them with protecting his secret by quietly passing it on from generation to generation. During their years in Jerusalem, the Priory learned of a stash of hidden documents buried beneath the ruins of Herod's temple, which had been built atop the earlier ruins of Solomon's Temple. These documents... corroborated Godefroi's powerful secret and were so explosive in nature that the Church would stop at nothing to get them (*DVC,* 171).

---

[9] Picknett and Prince, *The Templar Revelation: Secret Guardians of the True Identity of Christ,* 338–9, 341.
[10] Ibid.
[11] The information in parentheses denotes a direct quotation and refers to the page number where the quote appears in *Angels and Demons* (*A&D*), *The Da Vinci Code* (*DVC*), or the movie (D*VC*: the Movie).

- In order to retrieve the documents from within the ruins, the Priory created a military arm—a group of nine knights called the Order of the Poor Knights of Christ and the Temple of Solomon ... More commonly known as the Knights Templar (*DVC*, 171).
- The Priory has a well-documented history of reverence for the sacred feminine ... it is a modern goddess worship society, keepers of the Grail, and guardians of ancient documents (*DVC*, 122, 315).
- The modern Priory of Sion has a momentous duty. Theirs is a threefold charge. The brotherhood must protect the Sangreal documents. They must protect the tomb of Mary Magdalene. And, of course, they must nurture and protect the bloodline of Christ—those few members of the royal Merovingian bloodline who have survived into modern times (*DVC*, 279).
- The Sangreal documents ... allegedly contain proof that Jesus had a royal bloodline (*DVC*, 270).
- The word Sangreal derives from San Greal—or Holy Grail. But in its most ancient form, the word Sangreal was divided in a different spot ... Sang Real literally meant Royal Blood (*DVC*, 271).

On page 269, Brown claims that Mary Magdalene was of the House of Benjamin and therefore she was of royal descent. He writes that "the Book of Matthew tells us that Jesus was of the House of David. A descendent of King Solomon—King of the Jews" (270).

- By marrying into the powerful House of Benjamin, Jesus fused two royal bloodlines, creating a potent political union with the potential of making a legitimate claim to the throne and restoring the line of kings as it was under Solomon (*DVC*, 270).
- The legend of the Holy Grail is a legend about royal blood. When Grail legend speaks of 'the chalice that held the blood of Christ' ... it speaks, in fact, of Mary Magdalene—the female womb that carried Jesus' royal bloodline (*DVC*, 270).
- Mary Magdalene was pregnant at the time of the crucifixion. For the safety of Christ's unborn child, she had no choice but to flee to the Holy Land. With the help of Jesus' trusted uncle, Joseph of Arimathea, Mary Magdalene secretly traveled to France, then known

as Gaul. There she found safe refuge in the Jewish community. It was here in France that she gave birth to a daughter. Her name was Sarah (*DVC*, 276).

The Truth about the Priory of Sion, the Dossiers Secrets, and the Royal Bloodline

From all of the above, it is clearly evident that Dan Brown has relied on *The Templar Revelation* and, in particular, on *Holy Blood, Holy Grail*. So much, in fact, that the BBC reported that Michael Baigent and Richard Leigh accused Brown of using *Holy Blood's* central themes.[12] Brown also admitted to using *Holy Blood, Holy Grail* as one of several sources while writing his book, saying: "I went out of my way to mention them for being the ones who brought the theory to mainstream attention … I have never been shy about saying *Holy Blood, Holy Grail* is part of this."[13] So while it probably cannot be said that Brown has plagiarized, it can still be said that he did take ideas from *Holy Blood, Holy Grail*. Interestingly, Richard Leigh has conceded that their own work has copied ideas put forward by others in previous books![14]

On the back cover of *Holy Blood, Holy Grail*, Baigent et al. state that their book is "meticulously researched" but the entire work has been proven to be based on a grand hoax. Paul Smith, a Priory of Sion expert, explains the fraud in detail on his website; the following excerpt is a summary of the *truth* about the Priory of Sion:

> The history of the Priory of Sion is unexciting and quite bland — originally formed in 1956 by Pierre Plantard and another individual as an organisation devoted to the cause of Low Cost Housing and attacking the planning developers of Annemasse (the town where Pierre Plantard lived during the 1950s), it was named after a local mountain called Mont Sion … Pierre Plantard, the person involved in the formation of the Priory of Sion served time

[12] BBC, "Court Rejects Da Vinci Copy Claim."
[13] BBC, "Brown Vindicated by Code Ruling."
[14] BBC, "Brown Vindicated by Code Ruling."

in prison during 1953 for abuse of trust... The Priory of Sion itself terminated sometime after August 1956 when Plantard served another time in prison between December 1956 and December 1957 over allegations relating to "corruption of minors."

During the early 1960s Pierre Plantard made the acquaintance of French author Gérard de Sède, and embarked upon a literary deal with him writing about the castle of Gisors located in the Normandy region of France — it was during this period of time — the early 1960s — that Pierre Plantard began claiming that the Priory of Sion originated in the Crusader period Jerusalem — claiming a link between his Priory of Sion and the religious order of the Abbey de Notre Dame du Mont Sion (the history of this latter religious order is well documented and it had no links with Plantard's 1956 society, dying-out during the seventeenth century). It was during this period of time onwards that Plantard began creating a false pedigree about the Priory of Sion, later alleging that it was part of the Knights Templar and that it was the Guardian of the Merovingian Bloodline (Plantard also claimed he was descended from the Merovingian King Dagobert II from the early 1960s onwards, but in fact he was really only descended from a 16th century peasant who picked walnuts). Plantard later met and began collaborating with Philippe de Chérisey, a bit-part actor, amateur poet and surrealist who was interested in esoteric puzzles — and this created another aspect to the modern myth of the Priory of Sion that Plantard was involved in creating — de Chérisey's input inspired by surrealist elements.

As for the 1967 *Dossiers Secrets* — Plantard first began fabricating bogus genealogies when he first met Gérard de Sède — and these genealogies were included in documents that contained his signature, showing that they were his fabrications. Plantard used the exactly same stencil-kit when he fabricated the *Dossiers Secrets* — proving that the *Dossiers Secrets* in the Bibliothèque Nationale were his fabrication. As for the Grand Masters List of the Priory of Sion — that too was an invention — but Plantard copied that list of names for his *Dossiers Secrets* from another source — during the early 1960s a French Mystic named Raymond Bernard formed a neo-Templar group and he compiled a List of Names that Plantard later simply added into his *Dossiers Secrets* claiming they were the Grand Masters of the Priory of Sion. One additional name was included in the List that was missing from the one invented by Raymond Bernard—that of surrealist and poet Jean Cocteau—because of Philippe de Chérisey's interest in surrealism.

That the whole original Priory of Sion story was originally a myth fabricated by Pierre Plantard can further be demonstrated by the existence of letters dating from the 1960s and written between Pierre Plantard, Philippe de Chérisey and Gerard de Sede, showing that all three of them were engaged in a confidence trick with the intention of making money. These letters are in the possession of French researcher Jean-Luc Chaumeil.

During the late 1980s Plantard revised his myth of the Priory of Sion—rejecting and repudiating the earlier version he himself fabricated in the 1967 *Dossiers Secrets* and compiled a brand new List of Grand Masters and devising a new pedigree—claiming it was founded in 1681 in Rennes-le-Château by the Grandfather of Marie de Negri d'Ables…

In 1993 French Police ransacked Pierre Plantard's home and according to one individual who investigated the matter Plantard swore on oath that everything he claimed about the Priory of Sion was made up. Between 1993 and 2000 when Plantard died, there were no more allegations about the Priory of Sion, no more Priory Documents deposited in the Bibliothèque Nationale, and up to the time of his death Pierre Plantard lived a life of isolation and seclusion.[15]

Jean-Luc Chaumeil was the first to uncover the Priory of Sion hoax at the end of the 1970s, and says that he "explained to Henry Lincoln that this whole business was a deception."[16] Paul Smith confirms this stating:

> Michael Baigent, Richard Leigh and Henry Lincoln…were [not] willing to accept that Pierre Plantard was a confidence trickster and that the Priory of Sion was a hoax—despite being told these things in advance by French researcher Jean-Luc Chaumeil. Michael Baigent is still obsessed today by the existence of the Line of David, and he merely transposed his personal obsession in the Line

[15] Smith, "Da Vinci Code: Creating a New Age Version of Christianity?"
[16] Debraine, "Bestseller The Da Vinci Code is Based on a Deception."

> of David over Plantard's fake genealogies contained in the fabricated 1967 *Dossiers Secrets* in 1982. The authors of *The Holy Blood and the Holy Grail* never presented any reason, let alone evidence, about why there should have been a marriage between Jesus Christ and Mary Magdalene that produced children in the first place.[17]

Apparently, Baigent et al. were highly fascinated by Plantard—the supposed "true king" of France—and refused to accept that they were being deceived by him. On a humorous note, Jean-Luc Chaumeil stated: "I attended their first interview with him. It was really surrealist. They greeted him with the words 'Hello Your Majesty.'"[18] But as it turns out, Pierre Plantard—the man on whom the authors relied for credible facts—himself contradicted their work. In a France-Inter radio interview in 1982, Pierre Plantard stated: "*The Holy Blood and the Holy Grail* is a good book, but one must say that there is a part that owes more to fiction than to fact, especially in the part that deals with the lineage of Jesus. How can you prove a lineage of four centuries from Jesus to the Merovingians? I have never put myself forward as a descendant of Jesus Christ."[19] In other words, Plantard admitted that he was a descendent of Dagobert II, but he never admitted that he believed in any divine descent—this was the invention of Baigent, Leigh, and Lincoln. What is even more astounding, is that after all these years of trumpeting a holy bloodline theory, Michael Leigh recently confessed that their theory is only conjecture. In February 2005 on the U.K's *Channel4*, presenter Tony Robinson asked him the following question concerning the claim that Jesus Christ married Mary Magdalene and that they had children:

> **Tony Robinson:**
> Do we have any evidence that there was a child?
>
> **Michael Baigent:**
> There's none whatsoever—that's purely hypothesis on our part—but I think it's a plausible hypothesis—that the Holy Grail is the bloodline of David—and if Jesus and Mary Magdalene

[17] Smith, "Da Vinci Code: Creating a New Age Version of Christianity?"
[18] Etchegoin, "An Enquiry into the Sources of *The Da Vinci Code*."
[19] Smith, "Da Vinci Code: Creating a New Age Version of Christianity?"

had been married and she was pregnant with this child—"yes, she would have carried the Grail to France"—and I think this is the way that we need to look at this material—Is it true? I don't know—Is it plausible? Yes.

Tony Robinson:
So the inspiration for *The Da Vinci Code* and a whole Canon of secret Grail hunts is no more than a Big Guess…[20]

Evidently, what Brown has hailed as "FACT" in *The Da Vinci Code*, is not really fact at all: The Priory of Sion was not established in 1099, and it did not exist as a goddess worshipping society whose main purpose was to protect the true the secret of Jesus' alleged marriage to Mary Magdalene. The Knights Templar, therefore, were not their military arm, and there is no royal Merovingian bloodline or any surviving descendant of Jesus Christ. I will return to the topic of the alleged marriage between Jesus and Mary Magdalene later in this apology, and in addition, we will also see throughout what other trumped-up stories and ideas Brown has lifted from the sources mentioned. It has been established that the Knights Templar were in no way affiliated with the Priory of Sion, since the Priory of Sion did not itself exist. But nevertheless, Dan Brown has created other fabrications about this crusading order:

2. Dan's Deceptions about the Knights Templar

- [That] the Templars were created to protect the Holy Land [is]…a common misconception (*DVC*, 172).
- The Knights Templar were founded by the Priory of Sion to retrieve a collection of secret documents… Their true goal in the Holy Land was to retrieve the documents from beneath the ruins of the temple (*DVC*, 172).
- The Knights discovered something down there in the ruins… that made them wealthy and powerful beyond anyone's imagination… They took the treasure from the temple and traveled to

[20] Smith, "Michael Baigent Profile and His Book *The Jesus Papers*."

Europe, where their influence seemed to solidify overnight (*DVC*, 172).

- Nobody was certain whether the Knights had blackmailed the Vatican or whether the Church simply tried to buy the Knights' silence, but Pope Innocent II immediately issued an unprecedented papal bull that afforded the Knights Templar limitless power... With their new carte blanche from the Vatican the Knights Templar expanded at a staggering rate, both in numbers and political force, amassing vast estates in over a dozen countries (*DVC*, 173).
- The church had made some deadly enemies through the years—the Hassassin, the Knights Templar, armies that had been either hunted by the Vatican or betrayed by them (*A&D*, 155).
- By the 1300's... the Knights amass[ed] so much power that Pope Clement V decided something had to be done. Working... with France's King Phillipe IV, the Pope devised an ingeniously planned sting operation to quash the Templars and seize their treasure, thus taking control of the secrets held over the Vatican (*DVC*, 173).
- [Clement] claimed that God had visited him in a vision and warned him that the Knights Templar were heretics guilty of devil worship, homosexuality... and other blasphemous behavior... Pope Clement had been asked by God to cleanse the earth by rounding up all Knights Templar and torturing them until they confessed their crimes against God (*DVC*, 173).
- The Church accused the Templars of secretly performing rituals in which they prayed to a carved stone head... the pagan god—Baphomet... [He] was a pagan fertility God associated with the creative force of reproduction. Baphomet's head was represented as that of a ram or goat, a common symbol of procreation and fecundity (*DVC*, 342–3).
- On Friday, October 13 of 1307... countless Knights were captured, tortured mercilessly, and finally burned at the stake as heretics (*DVC*, 173).[21]

[21] The above quotations very closely parallel the information on pages 82 and 85

- Rossyln Chapel … stands…on the site of an ancient Mithraic temple. Built by the Knights Templar in 1446, the chapel is engraved with a mind-boggling array of symbols from the Jewish, Christian, Egyptian, Masonic, and pagan traditions … Rosslyn Chapel was a shrine to all faiths … to all traditions … and, above all, to nature and the goddess (*DVC*, 464, 467).

Brown claims that Templars designed female sexual symbolism into Gothic cathedrals to honour worship of the goddess and that a Gothic Cathedral's "long hollow nave … [is] a secret pagan tribute to a woman's womb" (*DVC*, 352).

The Truth about the Knights Templar

The real Knights Templar (as opposed to those falsely represented in *The Da Vinci Code*) were a military religious order founded in approximately 1118 by a knight from Burgundy named Hugh des Payens, and a knight from France by the name of Godfrey of St.-Omer.[22] No historical evidence supports Dan Brown's claim that the Knights Templar were not created to protect the Holy Land. In fact, the original purpose of the Templars was to defend the roads to the Holy Land, and to aid and protect new pilgrims who flocked to Jerusalem from all over Europe.[23] Uncharacteristically for Brown, he rightly calls the Templars "the Order of the poor Knights of Christ and the Temple of Solomon" (*DVC*, 171). The official name of the Templars was indeed "the Poor Fellow Soldiers of Christ and the Temple of Solomon, and this name was derived from their early state of poverty and from the section of the king of Jerusalem's — Baldwin II's — palace where they lived.[24]

During the 1300s, The Knights Templar did grow rapidly in wealth and in numbers, but this was not, as Brown asserts, due to blackmail or any

of *Holy Blood, Holy Grail*.

[22] Douglas, *The New International Dictionary of the Christian Church*, 956.

[23] Paul L. Maier, interview in *The Da Vinci Code Deception*, DVD.

[24] Douglas, *The New International Dictionary of the Christian Church*, 956.

underhanded deal with the Vatican. The Templars simply grew wealthy due to gifts from royalty and donations from pilgrims, and "their influence spread to include financial and banking operations in Europe."[25]

With the fall of Jerusalem in 1187 and the expulsion of all Christians from Jerusalem in 1291, the Knights Templar ceased to be a crusading order. They became an organization independent of secular authority and continued to acquire wealth. For this reason, in 1307, King Phillip IV the Fair of France acted against them. France was bankrupt at the time, and by destroying the Templars, he felt that he could acquire their land and money, as well as indirectly strike the authority of Roman Catholic Pope Clement V. On Friday 13th of 1307, King Phillip ordered the arrest of every Templar in the kingdom on charges of witchcraft, homosexuality, and heresy. They were not, as Brown claims, all burned at the stake on this day. After their arrest, the Templars were tortured into making confessions, and those who refused to confess or recanted their confessions were deemed guilty. By mid-1314, a total of 120 Templars had been burned or executed, including Grand Master Jacques de Molay, despite their protests of innocence. In 1312, under immense pressure by Phillip, Clement dissolved the order of the Knights Templar;[26] but contrary to what Brown tells us, Clement was not in any way involved with their arrest or deaths. Even *The Templar Revelation* and *Holy Blood, Holy Grail* correctly hold Phillip responsible for the murders of the Knights Templar.

Moreover, there is no consistency in the Templars' confessions about the Baphomet — the mysterious stone idol that the Templars were accused of worshiping. Most Templars did not actually believe in the Baphomet, so the reason for their inconsistent confessions is probably due to the fact that this information was extracted from them under torture. In other words, immense fear and the hope of release from excruciating pain caused the Templars to utter what their accusers wanted to hear. The online *Templar History Magazine* managed by Stephen Dafoe pro-

---

[25] Ibid.

[26] Ibid.

vides an excellent understanding of the Baphomet and its connection to the Knights Templar:

> Central to the accusations brought against the Knights Templar was that they worshipped an idol named Baphomet. This idol is said to have taken the form of a head or sometimes a black cat. The Fifth category of accusations states the following: V**. That the brothers practiced idol worship of a cat or a head.**
>
> That this one aspect of the Templars mythos, could generate so many theories as to its true origins is amazing. The interest in the Baphomet has survived over 600 years and taken many forms. The opinions on the Baphomet vary greatly from scholar to scholar and mystic path to mystic path. The purpose of this section is to shed some light on some of the theories and the connection, if any, to the Knights Templar.
>
> One thing that is certain is that writers of the nineteenth century were prone to believe that the Templars were Devil worshipping Occultists, while historians of the twentieth century were of the belief that the Templars were party to the machinations of a corrupt government and church. It remains to be seen what the common consensus of this century will be regarding the order. While twentieth century historians may have believed in their innocence, the Baphomet mythos did survive…
>
> The image of the Baphomet is as varied as the explanations as to its etymology… [Below is] a listing of some of the more common descriptions of it.
>
> - An idol with a human skull
> - A head with two faces
> - With a beard
> - Without a beard
> - With the heads of a cockerel
> - With the head of a man
> - With the head of a goat and the body of a man but with wings and cloven feet
>
> [The first to create]… an illustrative image of the Baphomet [was] the nineteenth century Occultist, Eliphas Levi… Levi's illustration… shows the more popular appearance of the demon, said to be a symbol of lust, generation and wisdom.
>
> - The head of the goat

> - The upper body of a woman (maternity)
> - Cloven feet
> - A pair of wings
> - A candle on its head
> - A symbol of revelation combining male sexual potency with the four elements and intelligence
>
> Theories on the etymology of the Baphomet are many. To some it is believed to be a corruption of the Moslem prophet "Mahomet" or in English Mohammed. The Templars fought along side Moslem Assassins during their time and it is held that they may have adopted Islamic beliefs. This doesn't really hold water to anyone familiar with Islam as the religion forbids all forms of idolatry.
>
> Another train of thought is that Baphomet is really a joining of two Greek words meaning absorption into wisdom. In either case the fact remains that the Templars were accused of practicing their initiations and rituals in front of a large idol of the demon Baphomet.
>
> How did this belief come to be? Since King Philip of France sought to own the vast Templar wealth, he…had the Templars captured and tortured. During these tortures they made many confessions, among these, the disclosure that they had worshipped an idol said to be the Baphomet. Were these claims true? Perhaps we'll never know. Jacques de Molay, who had earlier confessed his and the Templars guilt slowly burned at the stake insisting the order was innocent of all but one offence, that of allowing torture to cause them to lie and confess untruths.[27]

So it is evident that the Baphomet is a myth, and perhaps even a creation of the Templars. It is also clear that the Baphomet is not male, and is not a pagan fertility god as Dan Brown asserts. If Brown had considered this entire notion logically, he would have concluded that it is unlikely for warrior-knights, who took the monastic vows of poverty, chastity, and obedience,[28] to pray to a pagan god of fertility. But why does Brown go to so much trouble to mention the Baphomet? Quite plainly because of its androgynous nature, and its connection with fe-

---

[27] Dafoe, "Templar Myths: The Baphomet Mythos."

[28] Douglas, *The New International Dictionary of the Christian Church*, 956.

cundity. Any god, goddess, or myth, that carries even a subtle message of womanhood or the sacred feminine, for Brown, must be glorified and exalted as god!

Concerning the claim that The Knights Templar built Rosslyn Chapel—which is featured at the end of the *The Da Vinci Code*—this is another one of Brown's falsehoods. The chapel was actually designed by Sir William Saint Clair of the Saint Clair family, a wealthy Scottish noble family. Sir William was the third and last Saint Clair Prince of Orkney; and he was one of, if not the, wealthiest and most powerful lords of Scotland. Sir William was responsible for building the village of Roslin in which the chapel was built. He officially founded the chapel in 1446, and it took nearly 40 years to complete the chapel as we see today.[29] It is *according to legend only* that the Saint Clairs were linked to the Knights Templar; and there is nothing to suggest that Rosslyn is built on the site of an ancient Mithraic temple. In addition, Rosslyn Chapel is quite obviously Christian, and its walls are covered in Christian symbolism. The official Rosslyn Chapel website[30] briefly gives examples of some of the Christian symbols found on the chapel's pillars, walls, and ceilings, but the site does not mention any Masonic, Egyptian, or Pagan symbols. The carvings in Rosslyn include sculpted figures of the Virgin Saint Mary with the Child Jesus and the Eastern Kings associated with the birth of Christ; squares with five pointed stars symbolic of heaven; a dove with an olive branch on the roof; angels holding musical instruments; Abraham and Isaac; Samson; David; and the Crucifixion. Further evidence that Rosslyn is a Christian building, and not a shrine to the goddess, is the fact that it was originally a Roman Catholic church. We can be certain of this fact, because in 1590, the St. Clairs who were responsible for the chapel, had not yet succumbed to the Reformation and remained Roman Catholics. Being a Roman Catholic church, Protestants viewed it as a place unfit for church services and the administering of sacraments:

---

[29] www.maknap.com/MysteryTV/places/rosslyn_chapel/articles/ssro_02_history.html.

[30] www.rosslynchapel.org.uk.

> The Presbytery records of Dalkeith reveal that in 1589 William Knox, brother of John Knox and minister of Cockpen, was censured 'for baptizing the Laird of Rosling's bairne' in Rosslyn Chapel, which was described as a 'house and monument of idolatry, and not a place appointed for teaching the word and ministration of the sacraments.' The following year, the Presbytery forbade Mr George Ramsay, minister of Lasswade, from burying the wife of a later Oliver St Clair in the Chapel.[31]

The chapel was rededicated as an Episcopalian chapel by the Bishop of Edinburgh at Easter 1862.[32] Rosslyn was originally named the Collegiate Chapel of Saint Matthew, and today it is still known as Saint Matthew's Collegiate Church. It is a working church with regular services on Sundays, Tuesdays and Fridays. Saint Matthews is a member church of the Scottish Episcopal Church which is in full communion with the worldwide churches of the Anglican Communion; and belongs to the Episcopalian Diocese of Edinburgh.[33]

With regards to Brown's assertion that the Knights Templar built cathedrals to honour goddess worship, the Templars did indeed construct a number of fortresses and churches. Many of these are still in use; like the Temple Church in London[34] which features in *The Da Vinci Code*. However, we must quickly point out that none of these buildings resemble a woman's womb or any part of the female anatomy, and do not include any female sexual symbolism. This idea is one which Brown has lifted directly out of *The Templar Revelation* which states that "Sexual symbolism is even found in the great Gothic cathedrals which were masterminded by the Knights Templar."[35] But this is not true. Typical Gothic cathedrals are rectangular or cross-shaped; but they are not as Brown says, shaped like a woman's womb. In addition, Gothic archi-

---

[31] www.rosslynchapel.org.uk/history/history-pt3.html.

[32] www.maknap.com/MysteryTV/places/rosslyn_chapel/articles/ssro_02_history.html.

[33] www.rosslynchapel.org.uk/htm/location.html; www.rosslynchapel.org.uk/htm/church-services.html.

[34] *The Da Vinci Code Deception*, DVD.

[35] Picknett and Prince, *The Templar Revelation*, 384.

tecture is derived from Roman public buildings and not from Pagan temples.[36] So once again we see that Brown invents false ideas to propagate ridiculous theories that do not exist. In this case, he has presented falsehoods about architecture to support his notion that the Church has always worshipped the sacred feminine.

Thus, as we have seen, without the Priory of Sion and the Knights Templar as the guardians of the Priory's secret, the infrastructure of Dan Brown's entire theory for *The Da Vinci Code* immediately falls apart. Brown has drawn on selected sources, the sources themselves consist of lies and fabrications, the sources have taken their ideas from other sources, the sources contradict each other, and they even contradict Brown's theories. And so the whole thing can be described as one great, big, irritating mess.

---

[36] *The Da Vinci Code Deception*, DVD.

CHAPTER FOUR

God, Faith, and Religion

> He is a heretic who believes on another God, or receives another Christ than Him Who the Scriptures of the Old and New Testament manifestly declare, which announce without any obscurity the Father omnipotent...and His Son.[1]

1. Dan's Deceptions about the Lord God

- Faith does not protect you . . . Medicine and airbags . . . those are things that protect you . . . God does not protect you. Intelligence protects you. Enlightenment. Put your faith in something with tangible results. How long has it been since someone walked on water? Modern miracles belong to science . . . computers, vaccines, space stations . . . even divine miracles of creation. Matter from nothing . . . in a lab. Who needs God? No! Science is God (*A&D*, 174).
- "Matter . . . Blossoming out of nothing. An incredible display of subatomic fireworks. A miniature universe springing to life. He [Leonardo Vetra] proved not only that matter *can* be created from nothing, but that the Big Bang *and* Genesis can be explained simply by accepting the presence of an enormous source of energy."

  "You mean *God*?" Kohler demanded.

  "God, Buddha, The Force, Yahweh, the singularity, the unicity point—call it whatever you like—the result is the same. Science and religion support the same truth—pure energy is the father of creation." (*A&D*, 72).
- *Each of us is a God*, Buddha had said. *Each of us knows all. We need only open our minds to hear our own wisdom* (*A&D*, 484).

[1] *Treatise on Re-Baptism*, *ANF*, 5.675.

- "Do you believe in God?"

  Vittoria was silent for a long time. "Science tells me God must exist. My mind tells me I will never understand God. And my heart tells me I am not meant to."

  "So you believe God is fact but we will never understand Him."

  "Her," she said with a smile. "Your native Americans had it right."

  Langdon chuckled. "Mother Earth."

  "*Gaea.* The planet is an organism. All of us are cells with different purposes. And yet we are intertwined. Serving each other. Serving the whole." (*A&D*, 110).
- Pantheism [is] the worship of all gods, specifically pagan gods of Mother Earth … the dimensions of the Pantheon's main chamber were a tribute to Gaea — the goddess of the earth (*A&D*, 224–5).
- Religions evolve! The mind finds answers, the heart grapples new truths … God is not some omnipotent authority looking down from above, threatening to throw us into a pit of fire if we disobey. God is the energy that flows through the synapses of our nervous system and the chambers of our hearts! God is in all things!" (*A&D*, 534).

The Truth about the Lord God

The above quotes indicate two major problematic points: 1) that science is the only objective truth for humanity and 2) that God is simply a force or energy and a clear/particular understanding of Him is unnecessary.

1) The Holy Orthodox Church does not deny the importance of science and does not negate the necessity of scientific experiments and contributions throughout history. However, we would also say that there are things which science cannot explain, things which science cannot prove, and things before which science stands baffled—unable to comprehend. While the sciences may be an important element of our world and contribute to how we understand it, so is faith. Thus, Saint Paul the apostle writes of faith, in his epistle to the Hebrews: "Now faith is the

subsistence of things hoped for, a proof of things not seen."[2] We must concede that there are things which science cannot prove and therefore, we would have to argue that even science has its limitations.

Faith, then, goes beyond the bounds of the scientific and beyond the bounds of evidence and proof. Faith was the source of hope for many of the saints of the Church who gave up their lives for Christ, whether it be through martyrdom or by living in deserts and caves for the sake of their great love for Christ the King. Saint John Chrysostom writes that, "Faith ... is the seeing of things not plain, and brings those things not seen to the same full assurance with what are seen." It is necessary to emphasize that the Holy Orthodox Church does not reject science; however, She does not wholly depend on it for an understanding and explanation of all things since we are well aware of science's limitations.

2) Indeed, God is Creator of all things and He has taught us about Himself through the prophets of the Old Testament, and through His Only-Begotten Son Who was incarnate from the Holy Virgin Mary, taught us the means of salvation, and became our salvation through His crucifixion. Existent before the ages, God the Father abides in Perfect Love with His Son and the Holy Spirit. Brown makes claims that there may be several manifestations of God in forces, energies, ideas, etc., but our Orthodox understanding of God is not so vague and amorphous. The holy prophet Isaiah writes, "You are My witnesses, Says the LORD, and My servant Whom I have chosen: that you may know and believe Me, and understand that I am He: before Me there was no God formed, Nor shall there be after Me."[3] He is the only God and there are no gods before Him or after Him, for He is, indeed, the One True God.

Moreover, God the Father Who is eternal[4] has revealed Himself unto us, in time, through the Incarnation of His Only-Begotten Son

---

[2] Heb. 11:1.

[3] Isa. 43:10–11.

[4] When we say that God is eternal and exists in eternity, we mean that He is changeless and has no beginning and no end; that He has always existed; that He exists and continues forever; and that He is timeless, i.e. He Himself created time, is not subject to time, and is not under the count or limitations of time. The eternity

Jesus Christ and the gift and communion of the Holy Spirit. The Perfect Revelation of God the Father is through His Son and we learn about the Father through the Son. Christ teaches us to pray saying, "Our Father Who art in the heavens" specifically showing us that God is not Mother, but Father and that His Only Begotten Son — *not* daughter — is Jesus Christ. The Judeo-Christian faith, then, is not the product of human genius or invention, rather it is the revelation of God to humanity as Saint John writes in his first epistle: "That which was from the beginning, which we have heard, which we have seen with our eyes, which we have looked upon, and our hands have handled, concerning the Word of life — the life was manifested, and we have seen, and bear witness, and declare to you that eternal life which was with the Father and was manifested to us — that which we have seen and heard and declare to you, that you also may have fellowship with us; and truly our fellowship is with the Father and His Son Jesus Christ."[5] As Saint John explains, Jesus Christ, Who from the beginning and Whom we saw through the Incarnation, is not a force or an energy or woman. Gods' revelation to humanity was not haphazard or random since it was made in the Person of Jesus the Christ, so it is for that reason that we must totally reject these relativistic and demeaning notions of God as energy or force since He has revealed Himself unto us in a particular way. "Our God," writes Tatian, "did not begin to be in time: He alone is without beginning, and He Himself is the beginning of all things."[6] That is, our God is not the product of our own imaginings as Brown has depicted Him; our God is outside of time. However, in order for humans to understand Who God is — and in order for humanity to know our Creator without speculating about Him — He has revealed Himself unto us. So why should we be content with vague notions about God when He is the One Whom we have seen with our eyes and Whom we know?

---

of God is expressed poetically by David the Psalmist when he says: "Before the mountains were brought forth, Or ever You had formed the earth and the world, Even from everlasting to everlasting, You *are* God." (Ps. 90:2).

[5] 1 Jn.1:1–2.

[6] *Address of Tatian to the Greeks*, *ANF*, 2.66.

2. Dan's Deceptions about Duality and Dualism in the Godhead

- In the early days… we lived in a world of goddess and goddesses… Every Mars had an Athena. The god of war had the goddess of beauty; in the Egyptian tradition, Osiris and Isis… And now we live in a world solely of gods. The female counterpart has been erased… It's interesting note that the word 'god' conjures power and awe, while the word 'goddess' sounds imaginary (Dan Brown).[7]
- The ancients envisioned their world in two halves—masculine and feminine. Their gods and goddesses worked to keep a balance of power. Yin[8] and yang.[9] When male and female were balanced, there was harmony in the world. When they were unbalanced, there was chaos (*DVC*, 39–40).
- Early Jews believed that Holy of Holies in Solomon's Temple housed not only God but also His powerful female equal, Shekinah. The Jewish Tetragrammaton[10] YHWH — the sacred name of God — in fact derived from Jehovah, an androgynous physical union between the masculine Jah and the pre-Hebraic name for Eve, Havah (*DVC*, 336).
- The blade and the chalice. Fused as one. The Star of David… the perfect union of male and female… Solomon's Seal… marking the Holy of Holies, where the male and female deities — Yahweh and Shekinah — were thought to dwell (*DVC*, 481).

On page 130 of *The Da Vinci Code*, Brown further suggests that the face of Leonardo's Mona Lisa is androgynous, and that her name comes from two Ancient Egyptian gods—The male god Amon (the Egyptian god of fertility) and his female counterpart, the goddess Isis (the Egyptian goddess of fertility) "whose pictogram was once called L'ISA…AMON

---

[7] CNN, July 17, 2003.

[8] (in Chinese philosophy) the dark, not active, female principle of the universe.

[9] (in Chinese philosophy) the bright active male principle of the universe.

[10] The Hebrew name of God written in four letters, articulated as *Yahweh*.

L'ISA." Mona Lisa, Brown says: "is an anagram of the divine union of male and female."

The Truth that there is no Duality or Dualism in the Godhead

With regards to Brown's discussion of the feminine and masculine aspects of the Godhead, as we have already explained, God is not an idea, nor is He the product of human invention or of human desires. In the book of Deuteronomy, God teaches us that He is not a duality, "Hear, O Israel: The LORD our God is one LORD."[11] Thus, how can we believe Brown's claims that the Godhead is dual if God Himself teaches us otherwise through the prophets? The Holy Orthodox Church worships a Triune Godhead. The Godhead is made up of three Hypostaseis Who are co-eternal, co-essential, and co-existent: God the Father, God the Son, and God the Holy Spirit. In other words, the Father exists co-essentially and co-eternally with His Only-Begotten Son and the Holy Spirit. We must understand that God does not have a gender—He is neither male nor female—for those adjectives are used only for humans and animals; however, He is still Father for the following reasons: 1) God is Father because He is the Unorignate and the Origin of everything, even the Deity itself. 2) God is Father because He eternally Begets His Son—He is eternally co-existent with His Son which means that He never existed before His Son. If there is a Son, then there must be a Father and they eternally co-exist. We use the term Father, not because we have chosen to assign a gender to God, but because He is the Begetter of the Son in eternity. Regarding this point, Saint Gregory Nazianzen writes, "This is what we meant by Father and Son and Holy Ghost. The Father is **the Begetter and the Emitter**; without passion, of course, and without reference to time, and not in a corporeal manner. The Son is **the Begotten**, and the Holy Spirit is **the Emission**."[12] Finally,

[11] Deut. 6:4.

[12] Saint Gregory Nazianzen, *3rd Theological Oration* (*on the Son*): Article II, *Nicene & Post-Nicene Fathers: Second Series* (*NPNF*), 7.301.

we also do not deny that Jesus Christ, even though He existed eternally in the bosom of the Father, took flesh, became Man and was born of the Holy Virgin Mary. Therefore, we cannot deny that Jesus Christ was incarnate as a Man — not a woman. These imaginings of writers, such as Dan Brown, that God is male and/or female merely reduce God to the level of human beings and reduce the Creator of all things to the level of human relations. The Holy Orthodox Church rejects these inventions and does not assign a gender to God in the same way — God does not exist according to a gender as do created beings. God is Father insofar as He has Begotten His Son and He chose to reveal Himself to the whole of creation through the Incarnation of His Son Jesus Christ. As Saint John tells us: "The Word became Flesh and dwelt among us."[13]

On pages 257–8 of *The Da Vinci Code*, Robert Langdon and Leigh Teabing provide a description of the symbols for male and female. They explain that the blade △ is the original icon for male, while the chalice ▽ is the icon for female. But any Neolithic scholar or archaeologist will tell you that the so-called blade and chalice are not the original symbols for male and female. In fact, there were no "original" signs as such, but many signs[14] and they were never called the "blade" or the "chalice," and never even included any type of blade or chalice. Towards the end of the novel (480–81) we are told that the "Star of David" or "Solomon's Seal" ✡ is a fusion of these symbols — a fusion of male and female. Technically, the ✡ is universally called "the hexagram." It is a six-pointed star composed of two overlapping equilateral triangles, and it most commonly acknowledged as the sign for Judaism. In the Jewish religion, it is known as the "Star of David," or more accurately in Hebrew, "Magen David." This literally means "Shield of David;" and "tradition has it that this symbol was the official Davidic seal and that it was emblazoned on the shields of David's mighty men."[15] It is said to signify God as King David's shield or protector. The hexagram is also, but more

---

[13] Jn. 1:14.

[14] Liungman, Symbols '98 Encyclopedia. Accessed from *Symbols.com: Online Encyclopedia of Western Signs and Ideograms* at www.symbols.com.

[15] Phillips, *Exploring the World of the Jew*, 149.

rarely, referred to as "Solomon's Seal." During the holocaust, Jews were forced to wear a yellow hexagram in Nazi-occupied Europe, and since 1948, a blue ✡ has featured on the flag of Israel;[16] but the hexagram has never been used by the Jews to symbolize God in an androgynous union. However, there appears to be no consensus by scholars concerning the origin, evolution, and meaning of the hexagram. Some say that it was only adopted by the Jews as their primary Jewish symbol in the sixth century A.D., and prior to that time it was chiefly associated with magic.[17] Many claim that "alchemists of the Middle Ages used ✡ first and foremost as a general symbol representing the *art of alchemy* and secondly as a sign for combinations of *water* ▽ and △ *fire*."[18] Brown says that a merging of △ and ▽ represents the divine union of the male and female deities — Yahweh and Shekinah — in the Holy of Holies. He lifts this false theology from *The Woman with the Alabaster Jar* by Margaret Starbird who writes that:

> ... the archetypal symbols for male and female, the Λ and the V depict an ancient dualism that can be reconciled and used to form the age-old paradigm for wholeness. This visual image is logically the hexagram, the ✡ ... Recent research about the feminine aspect of God in the Hebrew tradition reveals that the Holy of Holies was the marriage chamber where the union of Yahweh, the unseen Holy One, with His feminine counterpart, the Shekinah, was consummated ... the sacred ✡ remained in the rabbinical tradition as the pre-eminent symbol for the Sacred Marriage, a promise of harmony and well being.[19]

Brown also takes the idea of God having a female counterpart from *The Templar Revelation* which states:

> The original religion of the Hebrews was ... venerating both gods

---

[16] Liungman, www.symbols.com/encyclopedia/27/2722.html.
[17] Menorah Ministries. Accessed at www.menorah.org/starofdavid.html.
[18] Liungman, www.symbols.com/encyclopedia/27/2722.html. Cf. also *About Alternative Religions*. Accessed at http://altreligion.about.com/library/glossary/symbols/bldefshexagram.htm.
[19] Starbird, *The Woman with the Alabaster Jar*, 159, 165.

> and goddesses. Only later did Yahweh emerge as the pre-eminent deity, and the priests effectively rewrote their history to erase ... the earlier worship of goddesses... Raphael Patai, in his major work *The Hebrew Goddess*, has conclusively demonstrated that Jews once worshipped a female deity. Among the many examples he cites of Hebrew goddess worship is that concerning Solomon's Temple: despite the tradition, it was not built to honour Yahweh alone, but also to celebrate the goddess Asherah.[20]

So what do Brown, Starbird, and Picknett and Prince mean by all of this? They quite literally mean that Yahweh was married to a goddess called Shekinah, just as Osiris married Isis to bring forth Horus, and just as the Hindu god Shiva has his female counterpart, Kali.[21] But of course, this is absurd. Nothing was more fundamental to Judaism than the belief in one God, and *one God alone*; and He did not have a female counterpart. And actually, the notion of attaching sexuality to deity was so detestable to the Jews, that the word "goddess" is non-existent in the Hebrew language.[22] Even one of Brown's sources—*The Gnostic Gospels*—which is in agreement with mostly everything that Brown says, contradicts him on this point stating that "the God of Israel shared his power with no female divinity, nor was he the divine husband or lover of any."[23] It should be noted that Solomon's Temple did not house Asherah, as attested by Picknett and Prince. Asherah was a goddess of the Canaanites, and actually, ancient Israel was warned by God to avoid all contact with the Canaanite religion and to erase all traces of it from the land in which they were to settle (see Ex. 23:23–33).[24] On the subject of the female goddess by the name of Shekinah; this is just one of Brown's creations. Shekinah, in fact, comes from a Hebrew word, and literally means "the in-dwelling presence of God" or "the presence of God dwelling." So when the Divine presence of God inhabited the Holy of Holies (particularly when resting on the Mercy Seat between

[20] Picknett and Prince, *The Templar Revelation*, 389–90.

[21] *A Lion Handbook: The World's Religions*, 184, 187.

[22] Paul L. Maier, interview in *The Da Vinci Code Deception*, DVD.

[23] Pagels, *The Gnostic Gospels*, 48.

[24] *A Lion Handbook: The World's Religions*, 64.

the Cherubim) inside the Tabernacle or the Temple of Solomon, the Jews called this the "in-dwelling of God;" "the in-dwelling" of His glory. Therefore, Shekinah really means "the glory of God is dwelling;" and it is not a female goddess.

The Tetragrammaton — YHWH — which is pronounced as Yahweh, is the very special, sacred name for the God of Israel. In Exodus, when Moses was speaking with God in the burning bush, Moses asked God:

> "When I come to the children of Israel and say to them, 'The God of your fathers has sent me to you,' and they say to me, 'What is His name?' what shall I say to them?" And God said to Moses, I AM WHO I AM." And He said, "Thus you shall say to the children of Israel, 'I AM has sent me to you.'"[25]

Yahweh (Jehovah) is a form of the Hebrew verb "to be," translated in Exodus 3:13–14 as "I AM." Early Christian author Clement of Alexandria affirms (ca. 195), "that mystic name that is called the Tetragrammaton … is pronounced Jehovah, which means, 'Who is, and who shall be.'"[26] So Yahweh (Jehovah) in Hebrew means "the present One, He Who is" or more precisely, "The Being." The earliest manuscripts of the Hebrew Bible contained only consonants with no vowels, so the sacred name appeared as YHWH. The Jews considered this special name of God to be so holy, that it should not be uttered, and so they substituted the Hebrew word "Adonai" (Lord) in public readings of Scripture in their synagogues.[27] Contrary to what Dan Brown claims, YHWH is not derived from Jehovah, rather it is Jehovah which was formed from YHWH. In the 16th century, Hebrew scribes and rabbis decided to form a new word — *Jehovah* — by taking the consonants YHWH (yōd hē wāw hē: יהוה) and inserting the vowels from Adonai (a–o–a) between them. This resulted in the word "Yahowah" (Yahweh) or "Jehovah." And since Jehovah comes from YHWH, Brown's claim that Jehovah is the amalgamation of the masculine *Jah* and the female *Havah* is proven to be false. As we have seen, Jehovah has nothing at all to do with an androgynous

[25] Ex. 3:13–14.

[26] Clement of Alexandria, *Fragment XII*.8, *ANF*, 2.585.

[27] Douglas, *The New International Dictionary of the Christian Church*, 527.

union. To say that Shekinah is God's female equal and that the word Jehovah is a derivative of an androgynous union, directly attacks Judaism and makes a mockery of its fundamental belief. This proves Brown's loathing for solely patriarchal religions, and confirms that *The Da Vinci Code* attacks Judaism as well as Christianity.

Concerning Dan Brown's assertions that Leonardo's painting of the Mona Lisa is androgynous, Brown, again, is incorrect. Although there is no conclusive proof of the identity of the woman pictured in the Mona Lisa, she is not — as Brown suggests — a self-portrait of Leonardo as woman. Brown's comment that "computerized analysis of the Mona Lisa and da Vinci's self portraits confirm some startling points of congruency in their faces" (*DVC*, 129) is quite ridiculous. There is no doubt that the Mona Lisa is, indeed, a woman; and actually she is thought to be Madonna Lisa—the wife of Francesco del Giocondo. Further, the name Mona Lisa is not a derivative of the words Amon and Isis, and it has no association with a divine union of any type. Madonna in Italian means "lady" or "madame," so Mona Lisa means *Madame Lisa*. And in truth, Leonardo did not even assign a name to this painting, or to any of his works; it was Georgio Vasari who gave the Mona Lisa its name in 1550 in Leonardo's biography.[28] Again Dan Brown insists on conveying a feminine pagan connection in his work, even if no such connection exists.

3. Dan's Deceptions about the Lord God's Power to Perform Miracles

- Does one need to believe in miracles to experience them? Mortati was a modern man in an ancient faith. Miracles never played a part in his belief. Certainly his faith spoke of miracles … bleeding palms … ascensions from the dead, imprints on shrouds … and yet, Mortati's rational mind had always justified these accounts as part of the myth. They were simply the result of man's greatest weak-

[28] *The Da Vinci Code Deception* DVD.

ness — his need for proof. Miracles were nothing but stories we all clung to because we wished they were true (*A&D*, 501).

- Holy visions and divine messages had always seemed like wishful delusions ... the product of overzealous minds hearing that they wanted to hear — God did not interact directly! (*A&D*, 477).

The Truth about the Lord God's Power to Perform Miracles

So as to inform the reader of the context for the above quotes, we will say in brief that, in *Angels and Demons*, Mortati, a fictional character, is a Roman Catholic cardinal who is the Vatican conclave's Great Elector or master of ceremonies. In *Angels and Demons*, Brown repeatedly casts doubts on God's authority to perform miracles and attempts to debase this concept.

How naïve and utterly superficial is it to claim that all visions and miracles are a product "of overzealous minds hearing that they wanted to hear." As we have mentioned above, science has its limitations and we must not deny the presence of an invisible world. To explain away the miraculous by claiming that miracles are psychological phenomena which take place because of human delusion is to undermine the presence of a spiritual realm; furthermore, it is to say that human beings are comprised of only mind and body — not souls or spirits. This is not the case. The human being is not simply mind and body, but also has a soul and spirit, through which s/he may interact with the spiritual realm of our world. This is not to say that all events are miraculous; the discerning soul must know that some miracles are in fact sent by God and many are, in fact, delusional. Many so-called miracles are the inventions of humans for whatever reason or, what is worse, the deception of Satan and his demons. The important thing to remember is that miracles, when they are performed by God, have a purpose and do not simply cause a disturbance or confusion. The miracle at Cana of Galilee, for example, was the first miracle performed by our Lord Jesus Christ. This miracle was a true miracle because it had many purposes: 1) Christ manifested His loving kindness towards the bride and the groom so that they would not be embarrassed before their guests; 2) The miracle points to the passion and death of Jesus Christ on the Cross and His Pure Blood which would be shed for the sake of the world; and most importantly 3) After Jesus performed this miracle at Cana of Galilee, Saint John the Evangelist tells us, "This beginning of the signs Jesus did in Cana of Galilee, and manifested His glory; and His disciples believed in Him."[29] Not only did the miracle have a practical side — the wine was finished before the wedding celebrations had ended — but there was an even greater purpose for this miracle and that was to manifest Christ's glory, to illumine the Divinity of our Lord God and Savior Jesus Christ, and for His disciples to believe in Him. It is not science or magic that converted plain water into the best fermented wine (as was acknowledged by those who tasted it at the wedding feast); but the Lord Jesus Christ, with His Divine power, authority, and humility, made the water into wine by His word.

While it is important to refute the idea that God does not perform miracles, we must also recognize that miracles which are from God have a purpose, such as the miracle at Cana of Galilee. Bleeding palms, on the other hand, are not recognized as miraculous occurrences by the Holy Orthodox Church for there is no purpose and no benefit from such a phenomenon. God is the performer of true miracles as we chant in the Midnight Psalmody: "Who among the gods, is like you O Lord? You are the True God, the performer of miracles." But we must be cautious for there are false miracles, just as there are false prophets. That which is from God is beneficial and allows us to believe in Him, just as the disciples believed in Christ.

4. Dan's Deceptions about Prayer

- Human beings normally use a very small percentage of their brain power. However, if you put them in emotionally charged situa-

[29] Jn. 2:11.

> tions—like physical trauma, extreme joy or fear, deep meditation—all of a sudden their neurons start firing like crazy, resulting in massively enhanced mental clarity... And yet remarkable solutions to seemingly impossible problems often occur in these moments of clarity. It's what gurus call higher consciousness. Biologists call it altered states. Psychologists call it super-sentience... And Christians call it answered prayer... Sometimes divine revelation simply means adjusting your brain to hear what your heart already knows (*A&D*, 484).

The Truth about Prayer

In other words, Brown describes answered prayer as a solution which results from enhanced mental clarity in emotionally charged situations. This wrongly implies that answered prayer is a result of our own understanding of a situation rather than God's intervention. The problem with the above mode of thinking is that it implicitly claims that human beings are self-sustaining and do not need aid from God or guidance from His Holy Spirit. If a human being simply needs to adjust his/her brain in order to hear what the heart already knows, that means the human being is individually capable of living without God—the Creator. But how can created beings forsake their Creator? How can created beings have life without their Creator? This individualistic and relativistic mode of thinking is very dangerous because it leads people to think that they can be their own spiritual guides, and it deceives people into believing that they are not in need of Divine assistance or guidance. But such thinking is quite normal for Brown, because he advocates a "do-it-yourself" religion where each individual is his or her own god and adheres to a personally tailored belief system.

The Holy Orthodox Church rejects this way of life and considers prayer as an extremely important part of the spiritual life in Christ. "No one is perfect, even if his life were but a single day on this earth,"[30] and

---

[30] From the litany of the reposed which is prayed during the Vespers service in the

for this reason we are always in need of God's grace and the direction of the Holy Spirit. Prayer in its deepest sense is a mode of life where one feels the presence of God in his/her life at all times. It is not necessarily speaking to God only when one is in need, but it is a conversation with God with every beat of one's heart. But for Dan Brown there is no God, and consequently there is no need for prayer. Of course, the topic of prayer itself is one of enormous depth, so it is not our place to discuss it in detail here. But in brief, Dan Brown's description of prayer presents God in a negative light since it eliminates God's omniscience and philanthropy. God knows the needs and requests of humankind even before they are uttered; and out of His great love for humanity He does hear prayers and responds to requests. In denying God's ability to do so, Brown presents to his readers a God who is weak and uncaring; static and unhearing. But despite what Brown says, we have the assurance that God hears our petitions and our cries particularly in times of despair, and indeed, at all times. As David the Prophet and Psalmist says: "Give ear to my words, O LORD, consider my meditation. Give heed to the voice of my cry, my King and my God. For to You I will pray. My voice you shall hear ... O LORD."[31] In many Psalms, David acknowledges that God has heard him. It is also important to note that God Himself explicitly declares that He can, and will, answer prayers when He says: "If you ask anything in My name, I will do *it*."[32]

The Holy Orthodox Church teaches that God answer prayers if we have complete faith that He is able to provide what we ask, and provided that our petitions are in accordance with His Divine and blessed will. We also believe that God answers our prayers in the time ordained by Him, and not necessarily at the time which we deem appropriate. We should understand that God is omnipotent; so if God does not provide what we have requested or is not swift in replying, this is not because He is incapable; rather it is because God, with His foreknowledge, chooses the most suitable time to respond our prayers and fulfill our requests.

Holy Coptic Orthodox Church.

[31] Ps. 5:1–3.

[32] Jn. 14:14.

There is much evidence of answered prayers by God in the lives of the Desert Fathers of the Holy Orthodox Church. Following is just one example:

> An old man had a servant who lived in village. Now it once happened that when the servant delayed to come according to custom, the old man was without what he needed, and when his delay was protracted, he lacked even what he needed for work in his cell. Vexed at not having what he needed, either for working or for eating, he said to his disciple, 'Will you go to the village?' The latter said, 'I will do as you wish.' Now the brother feared to go into the village on account of scandal, but he agreed to go so as not to disobey his father. The old man said to him, 'Go, and I trust that the God of my fathers will protect you from all temptation,' and saying the prayer, he sent him away.
>
> When he got to the village, the brother asked where the servant dwelt, and he found out. Now it happened that the servant and all his household were out of the village at the cemetery, except for one of his daughters who answered the disciple when he knocked on the door. When she had opened the door from inside and seen him, he asked her about her father, but she invited him to come inside, and even drew him in, but he refused. When she persisted for a long time, she ended by drawing him to herself, but seeing himself forced towards sin, and feeling that he was going to consent to his desires, he prayed with groans to God, saying, 'Lord, by the prayers of my father, save me in this hour.' At these words he immediately found himself on the river, returning to the monastery, and he returned unharmed to his father.[33]

So we disagree with Brown's notion that humans can solve their own problems without God's Divine assistance. We have confidence in the Lord Jesus Christ's words when He says to us: "Ask, and it will be given to you; seek, and you will find; knock, and it will be opened to you. For everyone who asks receives."[34] Moreover, we constantly call to mind the words of King Solomon the wise who said, "Trust in the LORD with all your heart, And lean not on your own understanding;

[33] Ward, *The Wisdom of the Desert Fathers*, 45–6.
[34] Matt. 7:7–8.

In all your ways acknowledge Him, And He shall direct your paths. Do not be wise in your own eyes."[35]

5. Dan's Deceptions about Faith and Religion

- Every faith in the world is based on fabrication. That is the definition of faith — acceptance of that which we imagine to be true, that which we cannot prove (*DVC*, 369).
- Since the beginning of time, spirituality and religion have been called on to fill in the gaps that science did not understand … Soon all gods will be proven to be false idols. Science has now provided answers to every question man can ask. There are only a few questions left and they are the esoteric ones. Where do we come from? What are we doing here? What is the meaning of life and the universe? … These are questions … [science is] answering (*A&D*, 25).
- Those who truly understand their faiths understand the stories are metaphorical … Religious allegory has become a part of the fabric of reality. And living in that reality helps millions of people cope and be better people (*DVC*, 370).
- Every religion describes God through metaphor, allegory, and exaggeration, from the early Egyptians through modern Sunday school. Metaphors are a way to help our minds process the unprocessible. The problems arise when we begin to believe literally in our own metaphors (*DVC*, 369).
- If you and I could dig up documentation that contradicted the holy stories of Islamic belief, Judaic belief, Buddhist belief, pagan belief, should we do that? Should we wave a flag and tell Buddhists that Buddha did not come from a lotus blossom? Or that Jesus was not born of a *literal* virgin birth? (*DVC*, 369).
- Religion is like language or dress. We gravitate toward the practices with which we were raised. In the end, though, we are all proclaiming the same thing. That life has meaning. That we are grateful for

[35] Prov. 3:5–7.

> the power that created us ... Faith is universal. Our specific methods for understanding it are arbitrary. Some of us pray to Jesus, some of us go to Mecca, some of us study subatomic particles. In the end we are all just searching for truth, that which is greater than ourselves (*A&D*, 110).

The Truth about Faith and Religion

The above argument suggests that religion, faith and truth are all relative. But why choose a particular religion (Christianity, Judaism, Islam, Buddhism) unless one believes that it is the truth? It seems almost useless to be an adherent to a certain faith and simultaneously believe that other faiths are all the same as your own. Such reasoning completely undermines any attempt to be a member of a given faith and, again, is a very individualistically driven mode of thinking. The Holy Orthodox Church acknowledges that the Truth is a Person: the person Jesus Christ, God incarnate — not a vague idea or a relative thought. He is the Truth and teaches us saying, "I am the way, the truth, and the life."[36] It is for this reason that we must reject this relativistic notion of religion and faith. Our faith is not a metaphor, for if it was we would undermine our very being: If Christ's birth from the Holy Virgin Mary, His Death, Resurrection and Ascension are all metaphors, then our faith is made a mockery and redemption is undermined. We cannot fall prey to the relativism upon which the above quotes rely. We do not believe in ideas or metaphors, we believe in Jesus Christ Who is a Person—God in the flesh Who emptied Himself of His Glory, took our form, and descended to our lowly state so that we might ascend with Him.[37]

The above quotes by Dan Brown describe religion in functional terms, that is to say that religion only serves a purpose in so far as it helps us to cope with our daily struggles and problems; if that is the case, it does not matter what kind of faith one has as long as one has a

[36] Jn. 14:6.

[37] This is the true story of God's Divine plan of salvation for the entire human race, which is outlined in more detail in Chapter Seven.

coping strategy. Saint Paul the Apostle speaks to this very point in his first Epistle to the Corinthians, when he explains that for those who believe the cross is power, but for those who do not believe — and say that it is a metaphor, fabrication or allegory — that it is foolishness: "For the message of the cross is foolishness to those who are perishing, but to us who are being saved it is the power of God. For it is written: 'I will destroy the wisdom of the wise, And bring to nothing the understanding of the prudent.' Where is the wise? Where is the scribe? Where is the disputer of this age? Has not God made foolish the wisdom of this world?"[38] Indeed, the so-called wise intellectuals of the age in which we live argue that it is not possible for our faith to be true, they make our faith out to be a mere coping mechanism, but this is not wisdom at all. They are limited to the capacities of their minds but we depend on the power of God.

[38] 1 Cor.1:18–21.

CHAPTER FIVE

The Church, Christianity, Constantine the Great, and Paganism

I owe my life and breath, my inmost secret thoughts to God.

The Emperor Constantine the Great[1]

1. Dan's Deceptions about the Church

In *Angels and Demons*, *The Da Vinci Code*, and in interviews, whenever Dan Brown refers to "Christianity" or "the Church" he specifically means the Roman Catholic Church. In *The Da Vinci Code*, he makes only one negative mention of the Church of England when referring to London's Temple Church saying: "Bleak... Church of England. Anglicans drink their religion straight. Nothing to distract from their misery." (*DVC*, 374); but otherwise he appears to have no awareness that other Christian denominations do exist. There is no mention of the Oriental Orthodox Churches, the Eastern Orthodox Churches, or even Protestant Christianity.

Furthermore, to add to his ignorance about the history of Christianity, Brown repeatedly refers to the Vatican in the fourth century in a negative light, and he confuses the Vatican and the Catholic Church as though they are one and the same. He often uses the term "the Vatican" instead of "Catholic Church."

- [Constantine established a] new Vatican power base (*DVC*, 253).

The Truth about the Church

Christianity, for Dan Brown, equals Roman Catholicism and is lo-

[1] Elliot, *The Christianity of Constantine the Great*, 134.

cated in Europe. This Eurocentric historical trajectory loses sight of the fact that European Christianity and Roman Catholicism are indebted to the foundations of the early Orthodox Church of the East (not the West). Within such an understanding of a westernized Christianity is lost any historical or religious tradition outside of Europe. This is not the fullness of Christianity. History and religion *do* exist outside of Europe and the world does not wait for Europe in order to understand Christianity. It would be a grave mistake to consider Brown's novels an accurate representation of the whole of Christianity and, even more, it would be a grave mistake to believe that Brown represents any form of Christianity with complete accuracy.

It was not until 1054 A.D. that the Roman Catholic Church split off from the rest of the Holy Orthodox Church and severed itself from its ties to Orthodoxy. By this time, the Holy Coptic Orthodox Church and the Holy Oriental Orthodox Churches in communion with Alexandria, were not in communion with the Chalcedonian Churches. Before 1054 A.D. there were five sees which were overseen by five patriarchs, although the patriarch of Alexandria was the first to be called Pope (Papa). The five sees, having apostolic lineage, were: Rome, Constantinople, Alexandria, Antioch and Jerusalem. The Patriarch of the See of Rome, because of his Petrine apostolic lineage, wanted to have full control over all five sees and this, of course, was rejected. As a result, Rome severed its ties from the Orthodox world and deemed its patriarch Pope (Papa). It is important to know the history of the Holy Orthodox Church because the Roman Catholic Church does not begin to exist until the middle of the eleventh century. Brown's representations of what he calls "the Church" is actually the Roman Catholic Church after the schism of 1054 A.D., *not* the whole of the Holy Orthodox Church. Furthermore, Brown refers to the Vatican in the fourth century, this is historically inaccurate since the Vatican did *not* exist in the fourth century. In Constantine's day, according to differing accounts by historians, the Vatican was either a swampy marsh or a cemetery on a hill. In the fourth century, technically there still wasn't even a Roman Catholic Church, but there was a universal Christian Church. Let the reader note, that the Roman Catholic Church is *not* "the Church" — for it comes into being after the east-west schism of 1054 A.D. — and that the Church was not governed by only one supreme power; rather, the governance of the early Church was divided amongst five sees. Of the five sees, we must note that the Church which had the most important impact on the foundations of Orthodox theology, Christology and doctrine was not Rome, but Alexandria. The Catechetical School of Alexandria made many important contributions to the Orthodox world with regards to theological articulations until 451 A.D. when the Coptic Church refused to accept the Council of Chalcedon's Christological formulations. Nonetheless, Orthodoxy and Christianity, in general, are indebted to Alexandrian fathers who defended and articulated the faith and it would be a historical fallacy to claim otherwise.

2. Dan's Deceptions about the Church as Evil

Whenever Brown refers to the Church or Christianity, he presents it as iniquitous:

- [Throughout history] the Church has killed to protect itself (*DVC*, 287).
- ... the Church has two thousand years of experience pressuring those who threaten to unveil its lies ... The Church may no longer employ crusaders to slaughter non-believers, but their influence is no less persuasive. No less insidious (*DVC*, 438).
- For two millennia your church has dominated the quest for truth. You have crushed your opposition with lies and prophecies of doom. You have manipulated the truth to serve your needs, murdering those whose discoveries did not serve your needs (*A&D*, 152).
- For two-thousand years, the Church has rained oppression and atrocity upon mankind. Crushed passion and ideal alike, all in the name of their walking God (*DVC*: the Movie).
- ... the Church had a deceitful and violent history. Their brutal crusade to "re-educate" the pagan and feminine-worshipping religions spanned three centuries, employing methods as inspired as they

were horrific (*DVC*, 134).

- As part of the Vatican's campaign to eradicate pagan religions and convert the masses to Christianity, the Church launched a smear campaign against the pagan gods and goddesses, recasting their divine symbols as evil (*DVC*, 41).
- Lies [were] spread by the church as a smear campaign against their adversaries (*A&D*, 37).
- The prostitute… Magdalene was no such thing. That unfortunate misconception is the legacy of a smear campaign launched by the early Church (*DVC*, 263–4).
- In the 1600's… *English* was one language the Vatican had not yet embraced. They dealt in Latin, German, even Spanish and French, but English was totally foreign inside the Vatican. They considered English a polluted, free-thinkers' language for profane men like Chaucer and Shakespeare (*A&D*, 217).

The Truth that the Church is Not Evil

Again the Holy Orthodox Church is not the Roman Catholic Church and the Roman Catholic Church is not the only church in existence! When we read about the Church or Christianity in Dan Brown's novels we must discern between his own imaginings and creation and what is historically accurate. By accusing the Catholic Church of smear campaigns, book-burning campaigns (*A&D*, 198), murder, a tradition of misinformation (*DVC*, 254), lies, suppressing the truth, and so forth, Brown blames all of Christianity as being responsible for events that they did not even have anything to do with.

Brown accuses "the Church" of the violence and the atrocities that took place during the crusades; however, we must note that not all of Christendom should be held accountable for the crusades, and neither did all of Christendom condone the crusades. We do not deny the fact that murder is unacceptable and cannot be justified whether it is done in the Name of Christ or not; there is no excuse for the violence committed during the crusades and we pray that such events will never happen again. However, not all Christians participated or condoned these acts of violence. The Holy Coptic Orthodox Church, for example, did not participate in the crusades and Her Patriarchs went as far as to write encyclicals stating that our Christianity should not be conflated with those participating in the ruthless violence of the crusades.[2] As for allegations of the Inquisition, suppressing the identity of Mary Magdalene, and the persecution of English thinkers such as Chaucer and Shakespeare—these allegations *all* pertain to the Roman Catholic Church, not any other. It is not our purpose, nor is it our place, to defend the Roman Catholic Church here, but our point is a simple one: The Church did not commit these atrocities which Brown describes and if they are true, we must ascertain that it was a local group who called themselves Christian rather than the whole of Christendom. Furthermore, it is important to highlight that the Coptic Orthodox Church was the persecuted Church, not the persecuting Church. In the eras of martyrdom, hundreds of thousands Coptic Christians were massacred and the Church struggled to survive; and indeed, it is a wonder to many that She did. And so again, we emphasize: European history and religion is not the only history and religion in the world, and we affirm that such allegations cannot be imposed onto those who do not identify with European Christianity.

3. Dan's Deceptions about Monasticism

On pages 14–15 of *The Da Vinci Code*, there is a description of Corporal Mortification: We read of how Silas, the Monk who is a member of Opus Dei,[3] strips himself naked, and tightens a leather strap, studded with sharp metal barbs that cut into the flesh (known as a *cilice*) around his thigh. He then flails himself repeatedly with a heavy knotted rope called *The Discipline*. "Exhaling slowly, he savored the cleansing ritual of his pain."

---

[2] Reference to these encyclicals is made in the *History of the Patriarchs of the Egyptian Church, Known as the History of the Holy Church.*

[3] Opus Dei is a personal prelature of the Roman Catholic Church that is negatively portrayed in *The Da Vinci Code.*

The Truth about Monasticism

Through his negative portrayal of the monk from Opus Dei, Dan Brown has completely destroyed the true image of monasticism. Monasticism is not about fear, pain, self-inflicted torture, or violence. Rather is a sublime life of prayer, of joy, and of hope. It is the life of being alone with the Lord Jesus Christ — the One who loves and who sacrificed His own life for us. It is a life where the love of God fills one's heart and where God alone remains in one's thoughts. The true monastic life includes unceasing prayer and silent contemplation on God and His beautiful, life-giving attributes. In true monasticism, the monastic becomes a partner with the angels and heavenly orders in praising the Almighty God, the Lord of Hosts. Indeed, monasticism is an angelic way of life, and the path to Christian perfection. And for this reason, monks and nuns are called "heavenly humans" or "earthly angels." The goal of monastic life is God Himself, and so the monastic cries out to God with the Psalmist saying, "*there is* none upon earth *that* I desire besides You ... God is the strength of my heart and my portion forever."[4] The monastic strives to be united with God at all times. This goal is achieved through consecration of the senses out of love for the Holy One; and by spending one's time in worship, stillness, meditation, and praise. It is not achieved through physical violence or flagellation. When we examine the real characteristics of monasticism, what becomes increasingly evident is Dan Brown's deviation from the truth. Dan Brown's depiction of monasticism is frightening, exceedingly disturbing, and grossly inaccurate. Monastic life, in reality, is the opposite of what Brown describes. In true monasticism, "the "cleansing ritual of pain" is not the monastic's pleasure, but God Himself is the soul's sweetness and satisfaction. The monk or nun feels entirely satisfied by the Living God who fills his/her life with every good thing; so much so, that the monastic feels that s/he is lacking nothing. We read of Saint Paul the first hermit, who dwelt in the inner desert for seventy years without seeing another human being.

[4] Ps. 73:25, 26.

He was able to live in this manner because God filled his entire life, and so he did not require anyone or anything else. Therefore, in monastic life the monk or nun daily experiences inner peace, calmness, and happiness, and not inner turmoil or fear due to the prospect of violent corporal mortification.

It was said about Saint Abba Anthony the Great, the father of monasticism, that after a long period of living in seclusion he emerged as one victorious — being neither too weak from fasting and ascetic practices or too lethargic from a lack of movement. Saint Abba Anthony is the icon of monasticism that many monks and nuns around the world strive to emanate. His emergence from seclusions teaches us that moderation must be practiced, even in monasticism. As for Dan Brown's representation of the Opus Dei monk, he does not stand for all monastics or monastic practices. The Church of Alexandria is recognized through the entire world as the founder of monasticism, but She has not, at any time, advocated any form of self-inflicted physical violence. The purpose of monasticism is not to mortify the body to the point where harm is inflicted upon it, for the body is also a talent that has been given unto us by God and we must use it to glorify Him. Saint Paul writes in his first epistle to the Corinthians: "Or do you not know that your body is the temple of the Holy Spirit who is in you, whom you have from God, and you are not your own? For you were bought at a price; therefore glorify God in your body and in your spirit, which are God's."[5] Therefore, we would reject this depiction of monasticism, for it is incumbent, *even* upon the monastic, to glorify God in his/her body and spirit. Asceticism is not a mortification of the body which deadens, deforms, or mutilates the body, for this body is a temple of the Holy Spirit and is not evil. We must sanctify our bodies, minds, hearts and spirits so that we may be for Christ in every way. Through His Incarnation, Jesus Christ has blessed and re-created our humanity, it is not for us to mutilate and torture that which God Himself has blessed.

---

[5] 1 Cor.6:19–20.

4. Dan's Deceptions about the Church Not Being the Sole Pathway to the Lord God

- A recent *Scientific American* article hailed *New Physics* as a surer path to God than religion itself (*A&D*, 45).
- Establishing Christ's Divinity was critical to the further unification of the Roman empire and to the new Vatican power base... This not only precluded further pagan challenges to Christianity, but now the followers of Christ were able to redeem themselves only via the established sacred channel—the Roman Catholic Church (*DVC*, 253).
- A child of Jesus would undermine the critical notion of Christ's Divinity and therefore the Christian Church declared itself the sole vessel through which humanity could access the divine and gain entrance to the kingdom of heaven (*DVC*, 274).
- For the early Church... mankind's use of sex to commune directly with God posed a serious threat to the Catholic power base. It left the Church out of the loop, undermining their self-proclaimed status as the *sole* conduit to God (*DVC*, 336).
- The unification of science and religion was not what the church wanted... The union would have nullified the church's claim as the sole vessel through which man could understand God (*A&D*, 33).
- In paganism, women were worshipped as route to heaven, but the modern Church has a monopoly on that, in salvation through Jesus Christ... And he who keeps the keys to heaven, rules the world (*DVC*: the Movie).

The Truth about the Holy Orthodox Church as the Only Pathway to the Lord God

Brown takes these ideas from *Holy Blood, Holy Grail* which offers a strong criticism of Saint Irenaeus' assertion that the Church is the only pathway to salvation: "Deploring diversity, he maintained there could only be one valid Church, outside which there could be no salvation. Whoever challenged this assertion, Irenaeus declared to be a heretic—to be expelled and, if possible, destroyed."[6] Brown speaks disapprovingly of this notion of the Church as "the sole vessel" to God, but it is the truth: One cannot know God or attain salvation without the Church. Ironically enough, the complaint against Saint Irenaeus is that he does not allow for so-called diversity. Is diversity, believing in anything that one desires? Is diversity, faith without structure? This post-modern world in which we live has tricked us into believing that freedom is life without regulations or structure; however, lack of structure or regulation does not lead to freedom but chaos. The Holy Orthodox Church is not a regulatory power which suppresses our freedom, rather, She nurtures us and for this reason the Fathers have likened the Church to a mother. "Who is able to have God as his father, before he has had the Church for his mother?"[7]

The Holy Orthodox Church is our refuge from the struggles of this world and liberates us from the strife of passing tempests. Just as the ark kept Noah, his family and the animals safe from the flood, so does the Church keep us safe from the dangers of the world. However, there was only one ark which kept Noah safe, there were not several arks from which to choose and this is indicative of the fact that "[t]he one ark of Noah," as Saint Cyprian writes, "was a type of the one Church."[8] Furthermore, because there was only one ark — and it was only through the ark that Noah, his family and the animals could live — anybody outside of the ark perished. Likewise, as Saint Cyprian continues to explain, "The house of God is one, and there can be no salvation to any except in the Church."[9]

The Holy Orthodox Church, then, is an essential part of the spiritual life in Christ, for it is not only the House of God and it is not only where we may find comfort and protection from the struggles and strife of this world, but it is also where we may go for spiritual healing. The Holy Orthodox Church is a spiritual hospital and the only place where we may obtain remission of our sins by consistent participation

---

[6] Baigent, Leigh, and Lincoln, *Holy Blood, Holy Grail*, 364.
[7] Saint Cyprian, *Epistle LXXIII*, *ANF*, vol. 5, p. 388.
[8] Saint Cyprian, *Epistle. LXXV*, *ANF*, 5.398.
[9] Saint Cyprian, *Epistle. LXI*, *ANF*, 5.358.

in the sacraments of Baptism, Confession and Holy Communion. To abandon the Church is to abandon a healthy mode of spiritual living. To believe that one can live without the Church is pure arrogance and condemnation as Saint Ignatius writes: "He, therefore, that does not assemble with the Church, has even by this manifested his pride, and condemned himself."[10]

Finally, as we have mentioned above in response to Brown's condemnation of the communal spiritual life, the Holy Orthodox Church offers the believer a system of support and accountability. We the struggling Church on this earth, look to the victorious Church in the heavens and hope that we too may be victorious. The teachings and teachers of the Holy Orthodox Church are there to help us in our race towards victory, rather than to keep us from being victorious. Moreover, the Church is not for a select group of people, it is for all those who are in need of Her services and teachings. The Church is a light unto the world, and as Saint Irenaeus writes, She is indeed a garden planted in this world, bearing many fruits:

> The Church preaches the truth everywhere, and she is the seven-branched candlestick which bears the light of Christ. Those, therefore, who desert the preaching of the Church, call in question the knowledge of the holy presbyters... It behoves us, therefore, to avoid their doctrines and to take careful heed lest we suffer any injury from them; but to flee to the Church, and be brought up in her bosom, and be nourished with the Lord's Scriptures. For the Church has been planted as a garden in this world.[11]

Let us, therefore, be mindful of the essential nature of the Holy Orthodox Church and let us not be deceived by those who falsely claim that salvation may be found outside of the Church, for this is not the case. Those who claim that the Holy Orthodox Church is oppressive have been tricked by a fictitious notion of freedom and are not willing to commit themselves unto God in a serious way.

---

[10] Saint Ignatius, *Epistle to the Ephesians*, *ANF*, 1.51.
[11] Saint Irenaeus, *Against Heresies*, *ANF*, 1.548.

5. Dan's Deceptions about the Church and Women

- SO DARK THE CON OF MAN ... the Priory's tradition of perpetuating goddess worship is based on a belief that powerful men in the early Christian church "conned" the world by propagating lies that devalued the female and tipped the scales in favour of the masculine (*DVC*, 133).
- Constantine and his male successors successfully converted the world from matriarchal paganism to patriarchal Christianity by waging a campaign of propaganda that demonized the sacred feminine, obliterating the goddess from modern religion forever (*DVC*, 133).
- The power of the female and her ability to produce life was once very sacred, but it posed a threat to the rise of the predominantly male Church, and so the sacred feminine was demonized and called unclean. It was man, not God, who created the concept of 'original sin,' whereby Eve tasted of the apple and caused the downfall of the human race. Woman, once the sacred giver of life, was now the enemy (*DVC*, 258).
- [The] concept of woman as life-bringer was the foundation of ancient religions. Childbirth was mystical and powerful. Sadly, Christian philosophy decided to embezzle the female's creative power by ignoring biological truth and making man the creator. Genesis tells us that Eve was created from Adam's rib. Woman became an offshoot of man. And a sinful one at that. Genesis was the beginning of the end of the goddess (*DVC*, 258–9).
- [The] Church ... subjugated women, banished the Goddess, burned nonbelievers, and forbidden the pagan reverence for the sacred feminine (*DVC*, 259).
- Women ... are a huge threat to the Church (*DVC*: the Movie).
- During three hundred years of witch hunts, the Church burned at the stake an astounding five *million* women (*DVC*, 134).

The Truth about the Church and Women

Brown repeatedly refers to the Church as predominantly male, misogynistic, and an institution that subjugates women, but as we have argued above, 1) Brown's definition of "the Church" is very limited and in some cases fictitious and 2) when we refer to the Church we refer to her as our *mother* and honour the Church by likening Her role to that of a mother toward her children. Furthermore, it is a farce to believe that patriarchy was introduced by Christianity and Brown's homogenisation and romanticisation of "paganism" attempts to claim that societies were once matriarchal. Contemporary anthropologists and scholars of tribal societies have completely rejected the idea that the so-called primitive societies and cultures were once matriarchal, this simply is not the case and never was. The inequity between men and women that is found in many societies the world over is not a product of Christianity—because it existed before Christianity—and cannot be blamed on Christianity. Brown groups "paganism" into one category and makes sweeping generalizations about all pagan religions prior to Christianity—such as their matriarchal systems, honoring women because they gave birth, etc.—this kind of generalization cannot be taken seriously and we should not assume that all pagan religions honored women more than men. As one author confirms: "... this notion is so vaguely conceived that it approaches stupidity—What "pagans?" People who have worshipped multiple gods range from the ancient Greeks to Hindus to the Norse and the Aztecs, and their religions have little in common and are certainly not free from patriarchal values—the intention is hard to argue with."[12] *The Da Vinci Code Deception*, additionally states that:

> One of the assertions that Dan Brown makes very frequently in this novel... is that Christianity brought a suppression into the world of the worship of the goddess—of the sacred feminine. First of all, this isn't based on any kind of factual historical evidence at all. Yes, there have been many societies that have worshipped both gods and goddesses, male and female deities, and many of

[12] Miller, "The Da Vinci Crock."

> those cultures continued doing so after Christianity. The second problem is that it's a perspective that completely ignores Judaism. Judaism emerged of course, 3,000 years before Christianity [and] centered on a male deity — a male figure that was worshipped as God ... For Brown to ignore this is very strange, and for him to put all the blame on Christianity is strange as well.[13]

Having said this, we must clarify that the Holy Orthodox Church and the message of Christianity in general is not one of inequity. In Jesus Christ, there is no discrimination of persons whether it is because of gender, race, ethnicity, class, or anything else. The holy Apostle Saint Paul tells us that "neither is man independent of woman, nor woman independent of man, in the Lord."[14] In his Letter to the Galatians he also writes that "There is neither Jew nor Greek, there is neither slave nor free, there is neither male nor female; for you are all one in Christ Jesus."[15] However, just because there is no discrimination between persons in Christ — because we "are all one in Christ Jesus" — does not mean that we do not have our defined roles. Both men and women are saved in Christ Jesus, but that does not mean that men and women are the same; that is not the case. Men cannot be women and women cannot be men, their roles are defined and they cannot be blurred. The roles governing men and women in the Church are too often misinterpreted by people like Dan Brown as oppressive; however, the Church in Her wisdom has allotted and defined certain roles for each gender.

Just as we would also teach in Trinitarian theology that the Father is not the Son and the Son is not the Holy Spirit, the three are co-essential and make up the Godhead, but each has, and fulfils, His own role as part of the Godhead and they abide in Perfect Love. The same is the case with men and women according to the teachings of the Holy Orthodox Church, they are equal in essence but men are not women and women are not men — each must fulfill their defined role and abide in respect together.

---

[13] *The Da Vinci Code Deception* DVD.

[14] 1 Cor. 11:11.

[15] Gal. 3:28.

The Holy Orthodox Church magnifies women saints just as much as men saints, moreover, we magnify the Holy Mother of God who is above all the saints and is higher than the patriarchs, the prophets, the angels, and the principalities. We honour the Holy Theotokos because she was worthy to bear the Creator and cooperated with the will of God saying to the Angel Gabriel, "Behold the maidservant of the Lord! Let it be to me according to your word."[16] We do not simply magnify the Holy Virgin because she gave birth to Jesus the Christ, but we honour her because her purity and holiness made her worthy of bearing God. While Brown wrongly honors woman through sexual union, we honour the sublime virginity of the ever-virgin Saint Mary. Moreover, if it was through a woman — Eve — that Adam neglected the commandment of God,[17] it was also through a woman — Saint Mary, the second Eve — that Adam was restored to his first place once again, and redemption was freely given through Christ to men and women.[18] It is also important to note that Brown only makes two indirect references to Saint Mary as the mother of Jesus Christ, without mentioning her name, when he says: that Jesus was not born of a *literal* virgin birth (*DVC*, 370), and that she is "awkwardly posed sitting with Baby Jesus" in Leonardo's painting *Madonna of the Rocks* (*DVC*, 141). This is because to mention the honour of Saint Mary in his book would contradict his position on the Roman Catholic Church's hatred of women; but as we already know, Brown's understanding of "the Church" and Christianity in general is very limited and overly biased.

In addition to honoring the female saints of all varieties (martyrs, monastics, married people, etc.), just as much as the male saints, the

---

[16] Lk.1:38.

[17] The Holy bible does not state that Eve ate an apple from the tree of knowledge as Brown claims, but that she ate of its "fruit" (Gen. 3:6).

[18] From the Thursday Theotokia of the Coptic Midnight Psalmody. There are seven Theotokias — one for each day of the week. The Theotokias glorify the Theotokos (the Mother of God) and the mystery of the Divine incarnation and virgin birth. They also include symbols and prophecies about the Virgin Saint Mary, the carrying of Christ in her womb, and her giving birth to the incarnate God for the salvation of all humankind.

Holy Orthodox Church also has defined roles for women such as the role of the deaconess who teaches and offers services specifically for women. Also, we must not underestimate the service and importance of the priest's wife. Since Brown only considers the Roman Catholic Church, which has a celibate priesthood, he does not have any concept of the Holy Orthodox Church's priesthood. The priest's wife plays a significant role in the service of the congregation and she works alongside her husband — but again, each person's role is defined so as to avoid confusion.

The Holy Coptic Orthodox Church, for example, offers many social services to women in particular: we help women who are preparing for marriage, women who might be in abusive households, women who seek an education, etc. We do all that we can to retain the rights of women in society. So it is shortsighted and ignorant of Brown to maintain that Christianity is oppressive towards women because from an ontological, ecclesiastical, and social perspective women are considered important members of the Holy Orthodox Church.

Before we move onto the next point, I would briefly like discuss Brown's claim that the Roman Catholic Church burned at the stake five million women, in order to demonstrate how much Dan Brown has distorted history to support his false claims about the Church's hatred for women.[19] Firstly, scholars confirm that the number of people executed as witches between 1400 and 1800 A.D., totaled between an estimated forty thousand and a maximum fifty thousand. Secondly, not all those killed were women, and in fact, about twenty to twenty-five percent were men. Thirdly, most of these people were average citizens and not strong-minded, free-thinking women as Brown falsely describes. Fourthly, not all were burned at the stake — about half were given short sentences of execution, while the other half were killed in public by hanging or burning. And lastly, not all were executed by the Roman Catholic Church — some were killed by Catholics, some by Protestants,

[19] Brown further claims that midwives were killed for "using medical knowledge to ease the pain of childbirth." (*DVC*, 134). He takes this idea from Picknett and Prince, *The Templar Revelation*, 207–8.

some by the Puritans of New England, but most by governments.[20] Interestingly, *The Da Vinci Code* motion picture corrects the error made in the novel, by giving a figure of 50,000 for those killed in the witch hunts. However the film makes the same error as the book by stating that only women were the victims, when really both men and women were tried and killed for witchcraft.

6. Dan's Deceptions about the Emperor Constantine

- [Constantine] was a lifelong pagan who was baptized on his deathbed, too weak to protest (*DVC*, 251).
- In Constantine's day, Rome's official religion was sun worship—the cult of Sol Invictus, or the Invincible Sun—and Constantine was its head priest (*DVC*, 251).

The Truth about the Emperor Constantine

These falsehoods are taken almost verbatim from *Holy Blood, Holy Grail*:

> "The image of Constantine as a fervent convert to Christianity is clearly wrong. He himself was not even baptized until 337—when he lay on his deathbed and was apparently too weakened or too apathetic to protest."[21]
>
> [Constantine] appears to have had some sort of vision … the vision was of the sun god—the deity worshiped by certain cults under the name of "Sol Invictus," "the Invincible Sun" … The state religion of Rome under Constantine was, in fact, pagan sun worship; and Constantine, all his life, acted as its chief priest. Indeed his reign was called a "sun emperorship," and Sol Invictus figured everywhere.[22]

---

[20] Jones, "Case Study: The European Witch-Hunts, c. 1450–1750 and Witch-Hunts Today."

[21] Baigent, Leigh, and Lincoln, *Holy Blood, Holy Grail*, 366.

[22] Ibid.

We believe that the Emperor Constantine the Great facilitated the growth and establishment of Christianity because he was righteous and God fearing. Some argue that Constantine only made Christianity legal because it was in his best interests, and that his baptism on his deathbed is a sign of his insincerity towards Christianity. Others state that he postponed his baptism, because this was common practice in Constantine's day. People at this time thought it better to be baptized at the end of their life as they believed that serious sins committed after baptism would not be forgiven. But in reality, Constantine was not baptized against his wishes. When he felt his death approaching, he confessed his sins, laid aside his purple robe for a white garment, and was baptized. Constantine even said that he really had wished to be baptized in the waters of the Jordan River like Jesus Christ, but it was not the will of God.[23] So we can say that Constantine was "too weak" to travel, rather than "too weak to protest" to being baptized as Brown says. It is true that Constantine was pagan until early into his adult life, but he was not the head priest of any pagan religion, nor did he remain a lifelong pagan. Of Constantine's conversion from paganism to Christianity, we are quite certain. Fourth century scholar Eusebius of Caesarea was the first to recount the story in his *Life of Constantine*; and every history book and every historian since has related the same details. Michael Molloy briefly recounts the Emperor Constantine's conversion thus:

> [In 312, the Emperor Constantine] marched on Rome to unseat the pagan Maxentius...The city was considered impregnable and Maxentius' forces seemed safe within the city walls. But then a strange turn of events occurred. It was to have a result of historic proportions... That same day Constantine saw a vision. In the sky in broad daylight there appeared a pillar of light in the shape of a cross. On the cross were inscribed the words: "by this sign conquer." In a dream the following night Constantine was directed to prepare the labarum, a banner with the chi-rho (the first two Greek letters of the word Christ) monogram. His troops were also to trace these letters on their shields. Fighting under the labarum,

[23] Wace and Piercy, *A Dictionary of Christian Biography*, 209.

> he was told, his troops would be victorious… He accepted the vision in the sky and his dream as the calling of God… This event is often referred to as the conversion of Constantine to the Christian faith… But it is also possible that Constantine already had a degree of faith which was solidified by these miraculous signs.[24]

We must recognize that Constantine allowed Christians to practice their religion freely. He re-opened the churches and, as a result, Christians were no longer killed for the sake of their beliefs. This is, in and of itself, a great accomplishment for Christianity, and the Holy Orthodox Church honors the Emperor Constantine for his efforts to cease the persecution of Christians. The irony of people like Dan Brown's (and others') arguments against Constantine is that while they deem Constantine's religiosity insincere, they don't consider the fact that Constantine's legalization of the Christian faith stopped the mass murdering of Christians. It seems that such authors only complain when pagans (that is to say, non-Christians) are killed; however, when Christians are persecuted and the victims of violence, they take issue with Constantine's level of piety. This approach seems to be absolutely unfair and predisposed towards the non-Christian side regardless of the situation.

7. Dan's Deceptions about the Origins of Christianity

- Historians still marvel at the brilliance with which Constantine converted the sun-worshipping pagans to Christianity. By fusing symbols, dates, and rituals into the growing Christian tradition, he created a kind of hybrid religion that was acceptable to both parties (*DVC*, 251–2).
- Nothing in Christianity is original. The pre–Christian God Mithras — called the Son of God and the Light of the World — was born on December 25, died, was buried in a rock tomb, and then resurrected in three days. By the way, December 25 is also the birthday of Osiris, Adonis, and Dionysus (*DVC*, 252).

[24] Molloy, *Champion of Truth: The Life of Saint Athanasius*, 114–15.

- Transmogrification ... The vestiges of pagan religion in Christian symbology are undeniable. Egyptian sun disks became the halos of Catholic saints. Pictograms of Isis nursing her miraculously conceived son Horus became the blueprint for our modern images of the Virgin Mary nursing Baby Jesus. And virtually all the elements of Catholic ritual—the miter, the altar, the doxology, and communion, the act of 'God-eating'—were taken from earlier pagan mystery religions (*DVC*, 252).
- Christianity is filled with examples of sun worship ... Christianity did not borrow *only* from sun worship. The ritual of Christian canonization is taken from the ancient 'god-making' rite of Euhemerus. The practice of 'god-eating'—that is, Holy Communion—was borrowed from the Aztecs. Even the concept of Christ dying for our sins is arguably not exclusively Christian; the self sacrifice of a young man to absolve the sins of his people appears in the earliest tradition of the Quetzalcoatl (*A&D*, 243–4).
- Even Christianity's weekly holy day was stolen from the pagans ... Originally ... Christianity honored the Jewish Sabbath of Saturday, but Constantine shifted it to coincide with the pagan's veneration day of the sun ... To this day, most churchgoers attend services on Sunday morning with no idea that they are on account of the pagan sun god's weekly tribute—*Sunday* (*DVC*, 252).

The Truth about the Origins of Christianity

As we have come to expect, these claims, again, are not Brown's original ideas. They are taken from *The Templar Revelation* and *Holy Blood, Holy Grail*:

> Scholars have confessed themselves puzzled over the basic question as to why Christianity ... should have been the one to survive and flourish ... The secret of its appeal was that it was essentially a hybrid, a blend of certain aspects of Judaism and of pagan, mystery

school elements.[25]

> In the Egyptian heyday of [the Isis cult] … the greatest … celebration came on 25 December, when the birth of Isis' son Horus was commemorated — and then, twelve days later, on 6 January, that of her other son Aion. Both these dates have been taken over by Christians — the Orthodox Church celebrates Christmas on 6 January.[26]

> Christians may believe that statues of Mary and the baby Jesus represent an exclusively Christian iconography, but in fact the whole concept of the Madonna and child was already firmly present in the cult of Isis.[27]

> By an edict promulgated in A.D. 321 … Constantine ordered the law courts closed on "the venerable day of the sun" and decreed this day be a day of rest. Christianity had hitherto held the Jewish Sabbath — Saturday — as sacred. Now, in accordance with Constantine's edict, it transferred its sacred day to Sunday … The cult of Sol Invictus meshed happily with that of Mithras — so much so, indeed, that the two are often confused. Both emphasized the status of the sun. Both held Sunday as sacred. Both celebrated a major festival on December 25. As a result Christianity could find points of convergence with Mithraism.[28]

As in many other parts of his writings, Dan Brown has borrowed much of the information written by other authors which, in my opinion, further invalidates him as a writer, researcher and dependable source. Furthermore, this notion that Christianity is the invented tradition which depends on paganism is problematic for the following reasons: 1) Again, Brown groups all pagan religions into one category, when all pagan religions are not the same, do not believe the same things and, in some cases, have conflicting ideas about their god. How is it that the whole of Christianity borrowed from the pagan religions of the Egyptians, the Greeks, the Romans, the Aztecs and so on? The accusation itself is so vague because it is simply impossible for Brown make a

---

[25] Picknett and Prince, *The Templar Revelation*, 387–8.

[26] Ibid., 395–6.

[27] Quoted in Ibid., 99.

[28] Baigent, Leigh, and Lincoln, *Holy Blood, Holy Grail*, 367.

concrete point about particular historical events. 2) Brown claims that Christianity is the invented tradition which depended on "paganism" which begs the question: From where did the pagan traditions come? Surely, they were invented, not the Divinely revealed faith of Christianity. Athenagoras makes this same point when he writes: "The gods, as they affirm, were not from the beginning, but every one of them has come into existence just like ourselves."[29] Pagan religions are the invention of humans, whereas the Christian faith is the Divine revelation of God to humanity. 3) The above examples offered by Brown so as to prove the so-called similarities between Christianity and pagan religions are not all accurate; neither are they compelling comparisons. For example, when Brown mentions the comparison between the iconographic depiction of Isis carrying Horus and the Virgin Mary carrying the Lord Jesus Christ. It seems that depicting any mother and child — regardless of who the mother and child are — will include the mother carrying her child in her bosom. While it is true that Isis carries Horus in the same way that Saint Mary carries Jesus, the question remains: How else might mother and infant be depicted?

Another example is Brown's mention of the god Quetzalcoatl, who Brown wrongly ascribes to the Aztecs. Quetzalcoatl was not an Aztec god, but a Toltec god — according indigenous Mexican cosmogony — who was defeated by the Aztec god of war Huitzilipotchli. The Toltecs believed that their god, Quetzalcoatl, would come back and defeat the Aztec god and reinstate the fallen Toltec kingdom. Spanish chroniclers wrongly describe the Aztecs as practicing "god-eating" and cannibalism, but these points have been disputed by contemporary historians of Mexico. There is no evidence that the Aztecs or the Toltecs or other ancient groups practiced "god-eating" and to accept Brown's unprofessional conglomeration of delusions as factual and historical is not advisable since these points have been disputed and disproved by contemporary scholars. Furthermore, it is the pagan religions which imitated Christianity and Christian practices, and not

[29] Athenagoras, *A Plea for the Christians*, *ANF*, 2.137.

the opposite. The following quotes from various Church Fathers speak to this very point:

> The devil . . . vies even with the essential portions of the sacraments of God. He, too, baptizes some—that is, his own believers and faithful followers; he promises the putting away of sins by a bath of his own. Mithras . . . celebrates also the oblation of bread, and he introduces an image of a resurrection.[30]

> The enemy, by his power, always imitates the forms of virtue and righteousness, not for the purpose of truly promoting its exercise, but for deception and hypocrisy . . . He is "transformed into an angel of light," ensnaring many by the appearance of piety.[31]

> The nations, who are strangers to all understanding of spiritual powers, ascribe to their idols the imbuing of waters with the self-same efficacy . . . For washing is the channel through which they are initiated into some sacred rites—of some notorious Isis or Mithras . . . We recognize here also the zeal of the devil in rivaling the things of God.[32]

On the point of Brown's claim that Constantine moved the Christian day of worship from Saturday to coincide with the pagan veneration day of the sun, this information is not accurate. In 321, Constantine did issue an edict requiring "rest on the venerable day of the sun" by the ceasing of public works, and the closing of law courts. But the reason for Constantine's decree was so that Christians would be free to worship on Sunday, and it had nothing to do with declaring a shift of the Christian Sabbath.[33] It should also be noted that prior to Constantine's edict, Christians had already considered Sunday as their holy day. Observance of Sunday as "the Lord's day" is mentioned in the Bible in Acts 20:7 and 1 Corinthians 16:2. It was called the Lord's day in commemoration of the Resurrection of the Lord who arose on a Sunday. Moreover, in the second century long before the time of Constantine,

---

[30] Tertullian, *Prescription Against Heretics*, *ANF*, 3.262–3.

[31] Methodius, *The Banquet of the Ten Virgins*, *ANF*, 6.349.

[32] Tertullian, *On Baptism*, *ANF*, 3.671.

[33] Douglas, *The New International Dictionary of the Christian Church*, 940.

church Fathers such as Saint Justin Martyr (ca. 110–165 A.D.) and Bishop Melito of Sardis (ca. 170 A.D.) referred to Sunday as the Lord's day in their writings.[34]

While Christianity is a new message and is not the product of human genius, but the revelation of God Himself to His Creation, it also incorporates concepts and ideas that may have been familiar to people from a cultural and historical perspective. This is not to say that Christianity borrowed from paganism, but it is to say that in order for the message of Christianity to be articulated within a cultural and historical context it did implement some concepts which were redefined in order to express its new theology. For example, the music and hymnology of the Holy Coptic Orthodox Church is mainly inherited from the ancient Egyptian tradition of music. We do not say that our hymns have simply been delivered to us by the ancient Egyptians and, of course, the content of the hymns has nothing to do with ancient Egyptian belief systems; however, the music itself was not invented by the Church but came from a long musical tradition in the land of Egypt. Needless to say, if Dan Brown had consulted a credible history book before making all the false assertions mentioned he would not have made such mistakes. But then again, it is hard to determine if Brown's errors are deliberate, or if they are the result of ignorance and lack of meticulousness.

---

[34] Ibid.

CHAPTER SIX

The Holy Bible, the True Gospels, and the Gnostic Gospels

But I make known to you, brethren, that the gospel which was preached to me is not according to man. For I neither received it from man, nor was taught it, but it came through the revelation of Jesus Christ.

St. Paul in his Epistle to the Galatians (1:11–12)

1. Dan's Deceptions about the Bible, the New Testament, and the True Gospels

- The Bible did not arrive by fax from heaven... The Bible is a product of man ... Not of God ... The Bible did not fall magically from the clouds. Man created it as a historical record of tumultuous times (*DVC*, 250).
- The New Testament is false testimony (*DVC*, 369).
- The New Testament is based on fabrications (*DVC*, 369).
- The Bible ... has evolved through countless translations, additions, and revisions. History has never had a definitive version of the book (*DVC*, 250–1).
- More than eighty gospels were considered for the New Testament, and yet only a relative few were chosen for inclusion — Matthew, Mark, Luke, and John among them ... The Bible, as we know it today, was collated by the pagan Roman emperor Constantine the Great (*DVC*, 251).
- Constantine commissioned and financed a new Bible, which omitted those gospels that spoke of Christ's human traits and embellished those gospels that made Him godlike. The earlier gospels

were outlawed, gathered up, and burned (*DVC*, 254).

THE TRUTH ABOUT THE BIBLE, THE NEW TESTAMENT, AND THE TRUE GOSPELS

The Holy Bible is not a product of man; it is the word of God. In the book of Jeremiah it is written, "The words of Jeremiah the son of Hilkiah, of the priests who were in Anathoth in the land of Benjamin, **to whom the word of the LORD came** in the days of Josiah the son of Amon, king of Judah, in the thirteenth year of his reign ... Then **the word of the LORD came** to me, saying: Before I formed you in the womb I knew you; Before you were born I sanctified you; I ordained you a prophet to the nations."[1]

Jeremiah was afraid when the Lord told him that he would be a prophet to the nations. He quickly replied, "Ah, Lord God! Behold, I cannot speak, for I am a youth. But the Lord said to me: Do not say, 'I am a youth,' For you shall go to all to whom I send you, And whatever I command you, you shall speak."[2] So, we see that it is God who sent the words to Jeremiah. The Lord then said, "Do not be afraid of their faces, For I am with you to deliver you, says the LORD. Then the LORD put forth His hand and touched my mouth, and the LORD said to me: Behold, I have put My words in your mouth."[3] The Lord did not want him to fear anyone; not even kings, because the words Jeremiah would speak were the words of God.

God continued to speak to Jeremiah saying, "See, I have this day set you over the nations and over the kingdoms, To root out and to pull down, To destroy and to throw down, To build and to plant."[4] This means that Jeremiah would not root out, pull down, destroy, throw down, build or plant with his own hand, because he was only a poor person. Rather, Jeremiah would do all of this by the words of his mouth,

[1] Jer. 1:1–5.
[2] Jer. 1:6–7.
[3] Jer. 1:8–9.
[4] Jer. 1:10.

which were really the words of the Lord. Such was the case with the New Testament. The authors of the New Testament were inspired by the grace of the Holy Spirit to write the Gospel and the Epistles. The problem with approaches like Brown's is that they are extremist, and so they either argue that the Bible has fallen out of the sky or that it is completely fabricated. We must understand that neither is true. Through Divine inspiration with the grace of the Holy Spirit, the Bible was written. Just as the above example shows Jeremiah's cooperation with the Son—the Word of God—and the Word of God working with Jeremiah, this is what occurred with the writings of both Old and New Testaments.

The New Testament does not consist of made up stories, legends, or tales, but it is based on eyewitness testimony. Saint Peter in his second epistle says: "For we did not follow cunningly devised fables when we made known to you the power and coming of our Lord Jesus Christ, but were eyewitnesses of His majesty."[5] Saint John also writes of "that which was from the beginning, which we have heard, which we have seen with our eyes, which we have looked upon, and our hands have handled, concerning the Word of life—the life was manifested, and we have seen, and bear witness, and declare to you ..."[6] So convinced were Saints Peter and John, and other eyewitnesses of the truth, that they paid the dear price of life for it; Christians were killed for their faith in the Bible. If the words of the Bible had been distorted, why would the martyrs have sacrificed their lives for a fabrication throughout the ages? No religion throughout the world, since its dawn, has endured as many persecutions or offered as many martyrs as Christianity. The Lord said, "I am watching over My word to perform it."[7] Was it impossible for the Lord to keep one version from being altered? If the Bible had been changed at some point in time, when was it changed? Where and what is the evidence for this accusation? As we will now see, it is obviously an unfounded accusation that is not attested to in the historical writings, nor is there any evidence of earlier versions of the Bible prior to this so-called change.

[5] 2 Pet. 1:16.
[6] 1 Jn. 1:1–2.
[7] Jer. 1:12.

The Da Vinci Code film goes a step further than Dan Brown stating that: "Constantine held a famous ecumenical gathering known as the Council of Nicaea; and at this council, the many sects of Christianity debated and voted on everything from the acceptance and rejection of specific gospels … to the mortality of Jesus."[8] But the idea that the Gospels were discussed at the Council of Nicaea is not true, and not original. It can be found in both *The Templar Revelation* and in *Holy Blood, Holy Grail*. *The Templar Revelation* states:

> … it was only in 325 CE that the Council of Nicaea met to debate which out of many books would be included in what was to become the New Testament. There is no doubt that the men present at the Council brought to the task their own prejudices and agendas, of which we are still reaping the sorry harvest. Eventually the Council established that only four Gospels would be included in the New Testament.[9]

And again: "The Council of Nicaea, when it rejected the many Gnostic Gospels and voted to include only Matthew, Mark, Luke and John in the New Testament, had no divine mandate for this major act of censorship."[10]

Holy Blood, Holy Grail says that Constantine:

> … sanctioned the confiscation and destruction of all works that challenged orthodox teachings — works by pagan authors that referred to Jesus, as well as works by "heretical" Christians … Then, in A.D. 331, he commissioned and financed new copies of the Bible…It was at this point that most of the crucial alterations in the New Testament were probably made and Jesus assumed the unique status he has enjoyed ever since. Constantine's commission must not be underestimated … The New Testament as it exists today is essentially a product of fourth-century editors and writers — custodians of orthodoxy, "adherents of the message," with vested interests to protect."[11]

---

[8] Direct quotation taken from *The Da Vinci Code*, a Columbia Pictures (Sony) release.
[9] Picknett and Prince, The Templar Revelation, 313.
[10] Ibid., 344.
[11] Baigent, Leigh, and Lincoln, *Holy Blood, Holy Grail*, 368, 369.

Brown's information, and that in the film, parallels the above in both sources rather closely; however, both are inaccurate. This contemporary notion of censorship is a very limited one and, again, the above authors impose a skewed sense of so-called freedom onto a historical context about which they are gravely misinformed. If the Emperor Constantine did actually tamper with the Gospels and suppress important books in order to further his own power and authority, why didn't historians, chroniclers or writers of the Late Antique period report on such an event? Why must we accept that the Gnostic gospels — which are deemed un-Orthodox — were once considered Orthodox articulations of the faith when, in fact, they were not? If ecumenical councils are held in order to define the faith, many teachings are bound to be rejected as un-Orthodox and some will be incorporated into the faith. Why then must Brown and others interpret the mere articulation of the Orthodox faith as a quest for power or something other than a desire to precisely define Christian doctrine? It is a contention that simply cannot be accepted. This returns us to the point that we have already made above: Brown and others who share his thoughts, believe that faith and religion should be vaguely articulated so that everybody is suited, and no one is offended. But above all things, Brown's thoughts about religion and faith assume that no one should have to change their thoughts, hearts, or beliefs for their faith — that faith should be accommodating and compromising. This is not freedom, this is chaos; and such vague notions about God lead to the worship of gods created by human invention. This is not the Holy Orthodox Church's posture on our Divinely revealed faith. The Gnostic gospels, as we will later see, were not included in the Holy Scriptures because their Christology did not coincide with what we have come to know as the canonical Gospels.

In further response to Brown's accusations of the Emperor Constantine's suppression of the Gnostic gospels, we must clarify that the first official list of books of the New Testament was penned by Saint Athanasius the Apostolic of Alexandria in his Paschal Letter of 367 A.D. This list contains the names of the books as they appear today in the Holy Bible. Saint Athanasius concludes his list saying, "These are fountains of salvation, that they who thirst may be satisfied with the living words they contain. In these alone is proclaimed the doctrine of Godliness. Let no man add to these, neither let him take ought from these."[12] However, the list had been well established by around 200 A.D., and evidence for this is provided in the writings of Saint Irenaeus. In 180 A.D. — more than 140 years before the time of the Emperor Constantine and the Council of Nicaea—Saint Irenaeus quotes from the four Gospels of Saints Matthew, Mark, Luke, and John as the *only true* gospels. Also, by the middle of the second century every book of the New Testament, had been referred to, at least once, as authoritative (canonical) by some of the apostolic Fathers.[13] Interestingly, a group of scholars conducted a study to determine what may happen if the entire New Testament were lost. They found that, from the writings of the holy Fathers of the second and third centuries, they were able reconstruct the entire New Testament, except for 11 verses. Moreover, the writings of the Anti-Nicene Fathers were investigated, and the scholars found that the total sum of citations from the New Testament was 36,289 — 19,368 from the Gospels, 1,352 from Acts, 14,035 from the Epistles of Saint Paul, 870 from the Catholic Epistles, and 664 from the Book of Revelation. This is further confirmation that the words of the Bible have never been changed.

Other proof that the Bible is not based on fabrications and false testimony can be found in disagreements which occurred in the early centuries of Christianity. The heretics argued with the saints, just as Arius argued with Saint Athanasius the Apostolic. As an example, Arius did not tell Saint Athanasius that the verses in the Holy Bible which proved that Christ is equal to the Father did not exist; but rather, Arius misinterpreted these verses and quoted other verses which he had also misunderstood. It is a well known fact that heresies appeared in Chris-

[12] Saint Athanasius, *Letter XXXIX (For 367.) of the particular books and their number, which are accepted by the Church. From the thirty-ninth Letter of Holy Athanasius, Bishop of Alexandria, on the Paschal Festival; wherein he defines canonically which books are accepted by the Church, NPNF*, 4.551–2.

[13] Geisler and Nix, *A General Introduction to the Bible*: Revised and Expanded, 288.

tianity since the first century A.D. Heretics, pagans, and Jews repeatedly misinterpreted the Bible, but never did they suggest that words in the Bible had been distorted.

There are many fragments, sections, or complete copies of original versions of the Bible in various museums all over the world. Yet it has not been found that any excerpt, even if only one page, differs from the Bibles that exist today. This fact elicits fundamental questions: If a person wished to alter the words in the Bible, how would s/he possibly collect all the versions or manuscripts from all over the world to affect the changes? And how could s/he collect all the copies of the Bible, after they had reached all corners of the world? Of course there are variants in versions of the Bible, but this is simply due to the nature of hand-copied manuscripts; it is inevitable that scribes would make minor errors. Many of the variants, for example, consist of missing letters or words (omissions), reversing of the order of letters or words (transposition), or errors in the spelling of words.[14] But such variants cannot, and are not, considered to be alterations to the Bible. Following are some examples of incomplete early versions of the Holy Bible which have survived to the present day:

- The earliest known biblical manuscripts dating to the closing centuries B.C. They include fragments of all books of the Hebrew Bible, except Esther, and a few portions of the Septuagint.
- The *Nash Papyrus*, dated between the second century B.C. and the first century A.D. This single leaf papyrus contains the entire Decalogue (part from Ex. 20:2–17, part from Deut. 5:6–21) and the Jewish confessional statement known as the *Shema* (from Deut. 6:4–9).[15]
- *The John Rylands Papyrus Fragment of John 18:31–33*, designated as *P. Ryl. 457* or *P52*, which dates from the first half of the second century, probably around 117–138 A.D. The fragment belongs to the John Rylands Library in Manchester, England.[16]

---

[14] Ibid, 469.

[15] Douglas, *The New International Dictionary of the Christian Church*, 694; Geisler and Nix, *A General Introduction to the Bible*, 358.

[16] Geisler and Nix, *A General Introduction to the Bible*, 388.

- *The Chester Beatty Papyri* which are portions of three New Testament manuscripts, designated as *P45*, *P46*, and *P47*. P45 dates to about 250 A.D., and contains the four Gospels and the Book of Acts. P46 also dates to about 250 A.D. and contains ten Pauline epistles and the Book of Hebrews. And P47 which dates to about 250 A.D. or later, contains the earliest extant text of the Book of Revelation, chapters 6–17. The papyri reside in the Beatty Museum near Dublin, Ireland.
- *The Bodmer Papyri*, designated as *P66*, *P72*, and *P75*. P66 dates to about 200 A.D, and contains the Gospel of Saint John (plate 1). P72 dates from late in the third century; it contains several canonical books and also is the earliest known copy of Jude, 1 Peter, and 2 Peter. P75 dates to the early 3rd century, and contains the Gospels of Saints Luke and John[17] (plate 2). All three papyri are housed in the Bibliotheca Bodmeriana near Geneva in Switzerland.

Examples of complete versions of the Holy Bible exist in the Vatican and in the British Museum—namely, the Vatican and the Sinaitic Codices. The Vatican Version, widely known as *Codex Vaticanus* (*B*), was written in Egypt in around 328–350 A.D. It is written in Greek in uncial letters, and is currently kept in the Vatican Library, Vatican City. The Sinaitic Version, known as *Codex Sinaiticus* (*Aleph*), was written around 340 A.D. on delicate parchment with four columns to each page. It was discovered by a scientist at Mount Sinai, and is currently housed in the British Museum. These versions contain the entire Old and New Testaments as we have them today. There are many more Bible manuscripts written after the time of Constantine, and they too are the same as our current version of the Bible. One such copy is the Alexandrine Version, known as *Codex Alexandrinus* (*A*) of the fifth century which is also kept at the British Museum. It may interest the reader to know that I have in my private library at the Monastery of Saint Demiana, authenticated copies of the Chester Beatty Papyri; the Bodmer Papyri; and the Vatican, Sinaitic, and Alexandrine codices; in facsimile/printed, photographic/

[17] Douglas, *The New International Dictionary of the Christian Church*, 216; 627.

printed, and microfilm/printed form. Also in the Monastery's library are official and authenticated copies of the *Aleppo Codex of the Whole Old Testament* and the *Leningrad Codex*, known as *Codex Leningradensis* (*B19*^{A}). The Aleppo Codex dates from around 930 A.D., and was written by Shelomo ben Baya'a but the vowel marks were added by Moses ben Asher. The Leningrad Codex was copied in Old Cairo by Samuel ben Jacob in 1008 A.D. from a manuscript written by Aaron ben Moses ben Asher in 1000 A.D.[18] Moses ben Asher and his son Aaron were Jewish scholars and the most famous Masoretes in the last ninth and tenth centuries. The Masoretes were scribes who codified and wrote down the oral criticisms and remarks on the Hebrew text. The ben Asher text is the standard text for the Hebrew Bible as it exists today, best represented by the Leningrad and Aleppo Codices.[19] Each of the manuscripts in the library at the Monastery of Saint Demiana was obtained officially from the respective libraries and museums where they are held.

The text in all of these manuscripts does not deviate from the text in our modern Bible. What is quite astonishing is that manuscripts, such as the Bodmer Papyri, match up with the texts in manuscripts, such as the Codex Vaticanus. The words are one and the same. So the words written by Saint John himself, for example, are the same words that appear exactly in manuscripts such as Codex Vaticanus, which are precisely the same words found in the Bodmer Papyri which are exactly the same words that appear in our modern Bible. What is even more quite astonishing is that the manuscripts were written by different scribes, at different times in history, and in different parts of the world; yet in spite of all of these factors they are all alike. Most manuscripts of the Bible were not available to us until the late 1800's so how can any person be accused of inventing or altering that which s/he did not even have access to? Thus it is plainly evident, that Brown's statement that the Holy Bible has evolved through countless translations, additions, and revisions is false, as is his statement that the New Testament is based on fabrications.

---

[18] Geisler and Nix, *A General Introduction to the Bible*, 358; *The Leningrad Codex: A Facsimile Edition*, xxix.
[19] Ibid., 371.

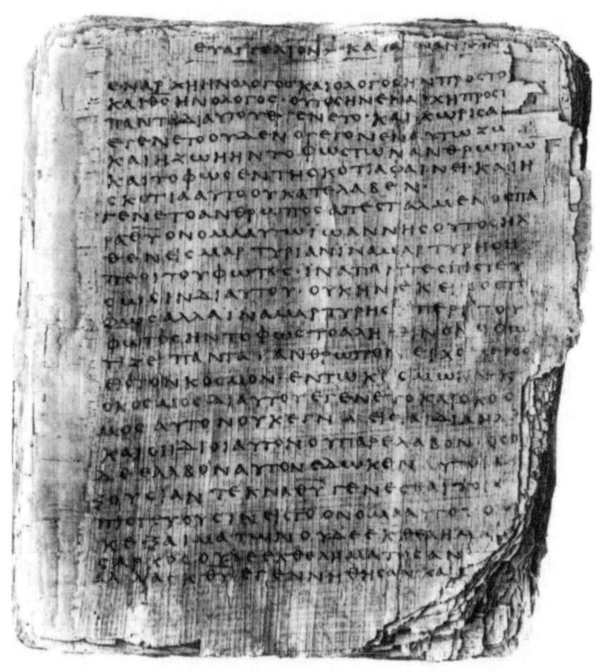

PLATE 1. Bodmer Papyrus P66, opened to John 1:1–14 (Bibliotheca Bodmeriana).

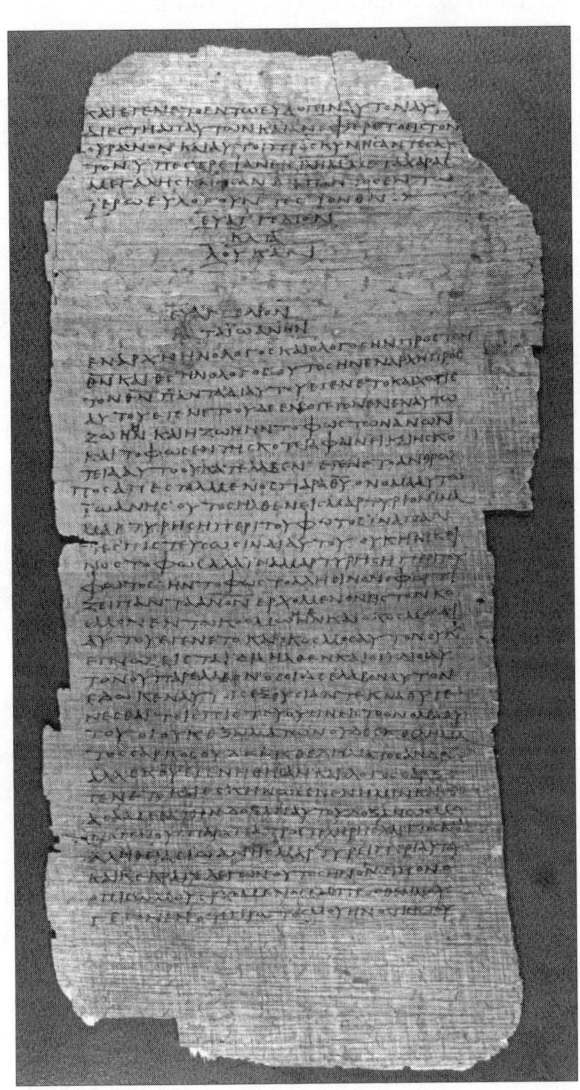

PLATE 2. Bodmer Papyrus P75, opened to Luke 24:51–John 1:16 (Bibliotheca Bodmeriana).

The Vatican and the Sinaitic Versions of the fourth century are both believed to have been written following an order by the Emperor Constantine the Great. Early Christian scholar Eusebius of Caesarea in his *Life of Constantine*, details how Constantine sent him a letter (ca. 328 A.D.) requesting fifty parchment manuscripts of the Scriptures for new churches which were to be built in Constantinople. Constantine's imperial request read:

> Victor, Constantinus, Maximus, Augustus to Eusebius ... I have thought it expedient to ask your Prudence to order fifty copies of the sacred Scriptures ... to be written on prepared parchment in a legible manner, and in a convenient portable form, by professional transcribers thoroughly practiced in their art ... it will be for you to take special care that they be completed with as little delay as possible.

These commands, continues Eusebius, "were followed by the immediate execution of the work itself, which we sent him in magnificently and elaborately bound volumes of a threefold and fourfold form."[20] Professor Bruce Metzger and Bart Ehrman further explain that:

> The suggestion has been made by several scholars that the two oldest parchment manuscripts of the Bible that are in existence today, namely Codex Vaticanus and Codex Sinaiticus may have been among those ordered by Constantine ... Eusebius' curious expression "volumes of threefold and fourfold forms" agrees with the circumstance that these two codices have, respectively, three columns and four columns on each page ... The most that can be said with certainty, therefore, is that Codices Vaticanus and Sinaiticus are doubtless like those that Constantine ordered Eusebius to have copied."[21]

So this request by Constantine was an order for copies of the Scriptures, it was not, as Dan Brown falsely states, an order for a "new Bible."

---

[20] Eusebius of Caesarea, *The Life of Constantine*, IV.36-7, *NPNF*: Second Series, 1.549.

[21] Metzger and Ehrman, *The Text of the New Testament: Its Transmission, Corruption, and Restoration*, 15–16.

As the word of God, we should hold the Holy Bible in high regard and treat it with due respect. The word of God enlightens our path, as it is written: "Your word is a lamp to my feet and a light to my path."[22] Both the Old and New Testaments are the basis for the Christian faith, and they did not emerge out of a vacuum as Dan Brown would have his readers believe.

2. Dan's Deceptions about the Dead Sea Scrolls and the Gnostic Gospels

- The early church needed to convince the world that the mortal prophet Jesus was a *divine* being. Therefore any gospels that described *earthly* aspects of Jesus' life had to be omitted from the Bible (*DVC*, 264).
- Some of the gospels that Constantine attempted to eradicate managed to survive. The Dead Sea Scrolls were found in the 1950's hidden in a cave near Qumran in the Judean desert. And … the Coptic Scrolls in 1945 at Nag Hammadi. In addition to telling the true Grail story, these documents speak of Christ's ministry in very human terms. Of course, the Vatican in keeping with their tradition of misinformation, tried very hard to suppress the release of these scrolls (*DVC*, 254).
- The scrolls highlight glaring historical discrepancies and fabrications … [in] the modern Bible (*DVC*, 254).
- The Nag Hammadi and Dead Sea Scrolls … [are] The earliest Christian records (*DVC*, 266).

The Truth about the Dead Sea Scrolls and the Gnostic Gospels

The Dead Sea Scrolls are *not* Christian records, they are Jewish documents which include Biblical fragments amongst many other Rab-

[22] Ps 119:105.

binic documentary fragments. The Nag Hammadi texts are not the earliest Christian records; rather, they may very well be the earliest known heretical writings which the Church rejected. The Gnostic texts are a group of writings that depict the Person of Jesus Christ as a human being, rather than as God incarnate; for this reason, the Fathers of the Church have rejected them as an un-Orthodox representation of the Christ. Saint Irenaeus in his treatise *Against Heresies* (ca. 182–188 A.D.) gives a full account of these heretical writings and why they do not coincide with Orthodox Christian Christological articulations. The reason that the Nag Hammadi collection has become fascinating to scholars is because the actual texts against which Saint Irenaeus was writing were now available for study — now the dialogue could be completed: Orthodox teaching vs. heresy. Just because these Gnostic texts were written in the Coptic language and just because they discussed the Person of Jesus Christ does not mean that they are, in fact, Orthodox Christological articulations. One of the main Christological problems that arises in most, if not all, of the Gnostic texts is the denial of Jesus Christ's Divinity. What Dan Brown considers a discussion of Christ and His life on Earth in "very human terms" is, according to Orthodox Christology and the Holy Orthodox Church, an utter denial of the fact that Jesus Christ *is* God incarnate. The authors of the Gnostic heresies were not able to comprehend how God could take flesh, become Man, and *still* remain God. This is because the pride of human thought cannot accept God's astounding humility. Saint Athanasius explains that Jesus Christ did not cease being God while He was on the Earth:

> When He moved His body He did not cease also to direct the universe by His Mind and might. No. The marvelous truth is, that being the Word, so far from being Himself contained by anything, He actually contained all things Himself. In creation He is present everywhere, yet is distinct in being from it; ordering, directing, giving life to all, containing all, yet is He Himself the Uncontained, existing solely in His Father."[23]

[23] Saint Athanasius. *On the Incarnation: With an Introduction by C.S. Lewis*, 45.

This is the Mystery of the Incarnation which the Gnostic heresies could not comprehend and it is for that reason that these texts depict Jesus Christ "in very human terms"—because they are not able to fully understand that "While He was still God, He became the Son of Man. But He remains the True God, Who came and saved us."[24]

3. Dan's Deceptions about the Q Document, the Gospel of Phillip, and the Gospel of Mary Magdalene

- Eyewitness accounts of the Sangreal treasure describe it as being carried in four enormous trunks. In those trunks are reputed to be the *Purist Documents*—thousands of pages of unaltered, pre-Constantine documents written by early followers of Jesus, revering Him as a wholly human teacher and prophet. Also rumored to be part of the treasure is the legendary "*Q*" *Document*—a manuscript that even the Vatican admits they believe exists. Allegedly, it is a book of Jesus' teachings, possibly written in His own hand (*DVC*, 277).
- Another explosive document believed to be in the treasure is a manuscript called *The Magdalene Diaries*—Mary Magdalene's personal account of her relationship with Christ, His crucifixion, and her time in France (*DVC*, 277).

In The Da Vinci Code Brown quotes excerpts from the Gospel of Phillip:

- And the companion of the Saviour is Mary Magdalene. Christ loved her more than all the disciples and used to kiss her often on the mouth. The rest of the disciples were offended by it and expressed disapproval. They said to him, "Why do you love her more than all of us?"

Brown then states:

- As any Aramaic scholar will tell you, the word companion, in those days, literally meant spouse (*DVC*, 266).

---

[24] From the Thursday Theotokia of the Coptic Midnight Praises.

He also quotes from the *Gospel of Mary Magdalene*:

- And Peter said, "Did the Saviour really speak with a woman without our knowledge? Are we to turn about and all listen to her? Did he prefer her to us? And Levi answered, "Peter you have always been hot-tempered. Now I see you contending against the woman like an adversary. If the Saviour made her worthy, who are you indeed to reject her? Surely the Saviour knows her very well. That is why he loved her more than us (*DVC*, 268).

The Truth about the Q Document, the Gospel of Phillip, and the Gospel of Mary Magdalene

Dan Brown's ignorance regarding the Gnostic texts is immediately exposed since he refers to Aramaic scholarship in reference to the Gnostic texts which—originally written in Greek—were translated into Coptic. Other writers have noted this same discrepancy in Brown's knowledge of his topic, one of whom is Laura Miller, who is equally troubled by Brown's misinformation:

> Some of Brown's mistakes are minor but telling. For example, his "Grail expert," Leigh Teabing, smugly declares that "any Aramaic scholar will tell you" that the word "companion" used in the uncanonical Gospel of Philip in describing Mary Magdalene's relationship to Jesus, "in those days, literally meant spouse." But…the Gospel of Philip is written in Coptic, not Aramaic, and the word in question is borrowed from yet another language, which is also not Aramaic, but Greek. And it does not mean "spouse" or "lover," but "companion," and is "commonly used of friends and associates."[25]

Brown's quote from the *Gospel of Phillip* is exactly the same as the one included in *The Templar Revelation* and *Holy Blood, Holy Grail*, except for the fact that both include at the end: "The Saviour answered and said to them, 'Why do I not love you like her?'" *Holy Blood, Holy Grail* also declares that "the word 'companion' is to be translated as 'spouse'"[26]

[25] Miller, "The Da Vinci Crock."

[26] Baigent, Leigh, and Lincoln, *Holy Blood, Holy Grail*, 381–2.

but *The Templar Revelation* goes further stating that "the original Greek word actually meant 'consort' or *sexual partner*"[27] and that the "Gnostic Gospel of Phillip ... specifically describes the Magdalene as Jesus' sexual partner." The *Gospel of Mary Magdalene* is mentioned numerous times by Picknett and Prince, while Baigent, Leigh, and Lincoln feature the same excerpt quoted by Dan Brown. Brown also draws on ideas in *The Gnostic Gospels* by Elaine Pagels.

The actual Gnostic text of the *Gospel of Mary Magdalene* omits the word *mouth*: "And the companion of the Saviour was Mary Magdalene. Christ loved her more than all the disciples. And used to kiss her on the ..." However, the Gnostic text of the *Gospel of Phillip* does not omit the word mouth. The film also includes a shortened version of the above quote from the Gospel of Mary Magdalene, but interestingly, it omits the word mouth from the Gospel of Phillip. Whether the word mouth is included in the manuscript or not, the Gnostic texts are not accepted by the Holy Orthodox Church and are not considered part of the canonical books of the New Testament. As we have noted, the reason that we do not accept these texts as part of our Scriptures is because their description of Jesus Christ does not coincide with that of the other Gospels or with an Orthodox Christian Christological articulation. It does not matter to us if the word "mouth" does not appear in the *Gospel of Mary Magdalene*; such a lacuna does not allow us to consider accepting the text since we do not deem it appropriate to describe the Lord of Hosts as a mere man who consorts with a woman. This is not our understanding of Christ.

As we have just explained, the Gnostic heresies attempted to deny the Divinity of Christ by depicting Jesus as a mere human; however, if the Divinity of Jesus is denied, His redemption of the human race would be deemed ineffective. How could a mere human redeem the human race? "What — or rather Who was it that was needed for such grace and such recall as we required? Who, save the Word of God Himself, Who also in the beginning had made all things out of nothing? His part it

---

[27] Picknett and Prince, *The Templar Revelation*, 83, 345.

was, and His alone, both to bring again the corruptible to incorruption and to maintain for the Father His consistency of character with all. For He alone, being Word of the Father and above all, was in consequence both able to recreate all, and worthy to suffer on behalf of all and to be an ambassador for all with the Father."[28] For this reason, we must reject these depictions of Jesus Christ as being a husband or sexual partner to Mary Magdalene, for how can the Creator of all things consort with His creation? How much is the gap between the Creator of the universe and His creation? Jesus Christ, Who is God incarnate, does not come to the earth in order to have a relationship with Mary Magdalene, nor does He become incarnate so that He may live in a human relationship with Mary Magdalene. No, this is not the case. Saint Athanasius clearly explains why Christ was incarnate:

> No, He took our body, and not only so, but He took it directly from a spotless, stainless virgin, without the agency of human father — a pure body, untainted by intercourse with man. He, the Mighty One, the Artificer of all, Himself prepared this body in the virgin as a temple for Himself, and took it for His very own, as the instrument through which He was known and in which He dwelt. Thus, taking a body like our own, because all our bodies were liable to the corruption of death, He surrendered His body to death instead of all, and offered it to the Father. This He did out of sheer love for us, so that in His death all might die, and the law of death thereby be abolished because, having fulfilled in His body that for which it was appointed, it was thereafter voided of its power for men. This He did that He might turn again to incorruption men who had turned back to corruption, and make them alive through death by the appropriation of His body and by the grace of His resurrection. Thus He would make death to disappear from them as utterly as straw from fire.[29]

Therefore, we must recognize that Christ became incarnate in order to deal with the corruption that had taken over the human race. In His own Body, He carried the sins of the world and died on behalf of the

[28] Saint Athanasius. *On the Incarnation: With an Introduction by C.S. Lewis*, 33.
[29] Ibid., 34.

human race in order to restore humanity to its first state once again. He did *not* take flesh in order to have a carnal relationship with Mary Magdalene or to have children with her, for this would completely undermine the Divine plan to redeem the human race. In Christ alone—the Word incarnate—we are saved, not through a human being. It is for this reason that the Gnostic heresies were fiercely rejected by the Holy Orthodox Church, because they denied the Divinity of Christ and the efficaciousness of His Incarnation, Death, and Resurrection.

Finally, with regards to the so-called "Q Document" which Brown claims is "a manuscript that even the Vatican admits they believe exists. Allegedly, it is a book of Jesus' teachings, possibly written in His own hand." The "Q Document" is *not* an actual document, but a hypothesis that assumes there must have been a document which the authors of the Synoptic Gospels (Saints Matthew, Mark and Luke) used while writing their own Gospels. The "Q" stands for the German word *Quelle* which means "source" and the hypothesis is based on the fact that there must have been a source which was referenced by the evangelists thereby making the three gospels synoptic. The problem with the "Q Document" theory is that it undermines our understanding of Divine inspiration by the Holy Spirit. We believe that the Gospels are the product of human and Divine cooperation. That is to say, the evangelists were inspired by the grace of the Holy Spirit to write their gospels; however, if we are to accept the "Q Document" theory, we replace Divine inspiration with a theory which presumes the presence of this document. If we are to accept the "Q Document" then we presume that the Gospels are the product of human invention based on a source which scholars imagine to have existed—of which there is no evidence. The Holy Orthodox Church does not accept this theory since its aim is to undermine the sanctity of the Gospels and attempts to make them out to be a set of writings like any other.

CHAPTER SEVEN

The Divinity of Jesus Christ and the Council of Nicaea

> We believe ... in one Lord Jesus Christ, the Son of God, begotten of the Father, only begotten, that is of the essence of the Father; God of God, Light of Light; very God of very God; begotten, not made; being of one essence with the Father.
>
> From the Nicene Creed, 325 A.D.[1]

1. Dan's Deceptions about the Divinity of Jesus Christ and about the Council of Nicaea

- Almost everything our fathers taught us about Christ is false (*DVC*, 255).
- Jesus was viewed by His followers as a mortal prophet... a great and powerful man, but a *man* nonetheless. A mortal (*DVC*, 253).
- Thousands of documents already existed chronicling His life as a mortal man (*DVC*, 254).
- Constantine upgraded Jesus status almost four centuries after Jesus' death (*DVC*, 254).
- Constantine needed to strengthen the new Christian tradition, and held a famous ecumenical gathering known as the Council of Nicaea... At this gathering... many aspects of Christianity were debated and voted upon — the date of Easter, the role of the bishops, the administration of sacraments, and, of course, the divinity of Jesus (*DVC*, 253).
- Jesus' establishment as the 'Son of God' was officially proposed and voted on by the Council of Nicaea... [and it was] a relatively close

[1] *The Nicene Creed*, *ANF*, 7:524.

vote at that… By officially endorsing Jesus as the Son of God, Constantine turned Jesus into a deity… whose power was unchallengeable (*DVC*, 253).

- The modern Bible was compiled and edited by men who possessed a political agenda—to promote the divinity of the man Jesus and use His influence to solidify their own power base (*DVC*, 254–5).
- It was all about power… Christ as Messiah was critical to the functioning of the Church and state. Many scholars claim that the early Church literally stole Jesus from His original followers, hijacking His human message, shrouding it in an impenetrable cloak of divinity, and using it to expand their own power (*DVC*, 253).

The Truth about the Divinity of Jesus Christ and the Council of Nicaea

Actually, it is quite the opposite: everything our fathers taught us about Christ is true. It is Dan Brown's Christology that is false. Again, Brown takes his ideas from *Holy Blood, Holy Grail* which states:

> Constantine… consolidated, in the name of unity and uniformity, the status of Christian orthodoxy. In A.D. 325… He convened the Council of Nicea. At this council the dating of Easter was established. Rules were framed that defined the authority of bishops… Most important of all, the Council of Nicea decided, by vote (218 for, 2 against. The Son was then pronounced identical with the Father) that Jesus was a god, not a mortal prophet.[2]

In responding to Brown's fabrications about the authenticity of the Divinity of Jesus Christ, and the true reason for the convening of the Council of Nicaea in 325 A.D., it is first necessary to present a sound Christological understanding of the Lord Jesus Christ, God incarnate, Himself.

The Lord, God and Savior Jesus Christ is the second Hypostasis (Person) of the Holy Trinity. God has One Essence in three Hypostaseis,

[2] Baigent, Leigh, and Lincoln. *Holy Blood, Holy Grail*, 368.

all equal in essence. The Hypostaseis share all of the attributes in the one Divine essence, and are characteristically distinct in the hypostasis. The *hypostatic attribute* of God the Father is that He is the origin or source, and the origin of Being in all eternity in relation to the other two Hypostaseis. The *hypostatic attribute* of the Son is that He is begotten of the Father in eternity as a hypostasis with true existence. By means of eternal generation, the Father is the Cause[3] of the personal existence of the Son within the Divine Being; the Son is inseparable from the Father as He is the Word of God. The *hypostatic attribute* of the Holy Spirit is that He proceeds from the Father as a hypostasis with true existence; He is inseparable from the Father as He is the Spirit of God. We say that the Father is God according to essence and origin, according to Hypostasis. The Son is God according to essence and is generated according to Hypostasis. The Holy Spirit is God according to essence and proceeds according to Hypostasis. The apprehension of the Trinity teaches us the eternity of the Three Hypostaseis (Persons).

The Lord Jesus Christ is called "The Word" in the New Testament. Saint John the Beloved Apostle in his gospel says: "In the beginning was the Word, and the Word was with God, and the Word was God."[4] This is a clear affirmation of Christ's Divinity. The term "The Word" (*Logos* in Greek) means the rational principle expressed in words. Therefore, 'The Word-Logos' means Reason, or Mind. Saint Gregory Nazianzen explains this saying, "He is called the Word, because He is related to the Father as the Word to Mind."[5] Saint Athanasius the Apostolic also speaks of "The Word" stating that:

> The Son is not a work of will, nor has come after, as the creation, but is by nature the own Offspring of God's Essence. For being the own Word of the Father ... He is Himself the Father's Living Coun-

[3] Being "the Cause" does not mean that the Father created the Son, but due to our limited human understanding, the word "Cause" is most accurate to describe how the Father generates or begets the Son from all eternity.
[4] Jn. 1:1.
[5] Saint Gregory Nazianzen, *4th Theological Oration (on the Son): Article XX, NPNF: Second Series*, 7.316.

> sel, and Power, and Framer of the things which seemed good to the Father... The Son of God then, He is the 'Word,' and the 'Wisdom;' He is the 'Understanding' and the 'Living Counsel;' and in Him is the 'Good pleasure of the Father; He is 'Truth' and 'Light' and 'Power' of the Father."[6]

Having explained that the Son is the Word of the Father, it is important to re-emphasize that the Father and the Son are two distinct Hypostaseis (Persons) who are inseparable. We must also recognize that there was never a time when the Father was not a Father, nor when the Son was not a Son; and there was never a time when they did not eternally coexist. Again Saint Athanasius explains:

> But just as a river, produced from a well, is not separate, and yet there are in fact two visible objects and two names. For neither is the Father the Son, nor the Son the Father. For the Father is the Father of the Son, and the Son, the Son of the Father. For like as the well is not a river, nor the river a well, but both are one and the same water which is conveyed in a channel from the well to the river, so the Father's deity passes into the Son without flow and without division. For the Lord says, 'I came forth from the Father and have come' (Jn. 16:28). But He is ever with the Father, for He is in the bosom of the Father, nor was ever the bosom of the Father void of the deity of the Son.[7]

Thus, the Son, the Logos of God, exists with the Father in eternity, and is Himself the Eternal God.

In his Epistle to the Hebrews, Saint Paul the Apostle says about the Lord Jesus Christ: "through whom also He made the worlds; who being the brightness of His [i.e. the Father's] glory and the express image of His [the Father's] person, and upholding all things by the word of His power, when He had purged our sins, sat down at the right hand of the Majesty on high, having become so much better than the angels."[8] The phrase

---

[6] Saint Athanasius, *Four Discourses Against the Arians: Discourse III, NPNF: Second Series*, 4.428, 429.

[7] Saint Athanasius, *Statement of Faith, NPNF: Second Series*, 4.84–5.

[8] Heb.1:2–4.

"express image of His person" means the image in which God manifested Himself in His Only-Begotten Son, and thus we could see Him in the Person of Christ. That is why Christ the Lord said: "He who has seen Me has seen the Father."[9] The Lord Jesus Christ was incarnate for our redemption to purge our sins. He gave up all of His glory although He "is the brightness of the everlasting light, the unspotted mirror of the power of God, and the image of His goodness"[10] and had made the worlds. Here the Apostle presents one of Divine attributes of Christ, as Him being the Creator. He created the world because He is the Logos — the Reason and Wisdom of God: "In the beginning God created the heavens and the earth. The earth was without form, and void; and darkness was on the face of the deep. And the Spirit of God was hovering over the face of the waters."[11] Therefore, Christ is not a creature, nor is He created because any creature cannot exist before its creation.

Christians have never denied the full Divinity and full humanity of the Lord Jesus Christ, the Logos incarnate. When our father Adam fell, his sin was directed against the infinite God; the penalty being eternal death. This bequeathed the human race with a corrupt nature resulting in recurring sin throughout successive generations. In this way, the sin of humanity became infinite in both quantity and quality. But through the Incarnation of Jesus Christ redemption was fulfilled. After the fall of Adam three main alternatives faced humanity: 1) God could have carried out His warning and put an end to humanity. But that would have meant God's defeat before Satan who had corrupted God's creation. If this had occurred, one could ask, why did God create man in the first place, if he was to be sentenced to death? 2) God could have forgiven humanity, for He is loving and merciful. But this would have meant that one of the perfections of God, namely love, would be magnified at the expense of another trait, namely justice. Furthermore, the problem did not lie only in forgiving the fallen human being, but in remedying the results of this fall, that is, the corruption of the human nature. What

---

[9] Jn. 14:9.

[10] Wis. 7:26.

[11] Gen. 1:1–2.

good would it be if God forgave us our past offenses without regenerating and sanctifying our nature, so that it might triumph over sin and enjoy fellowship with His Holy nature? and; 3) God could send a Redeemer to redeem us. Through this Redeemer the sentence of death would be executed on the one hand, and humanity would receive forgiveness on the other. And that is precisely what God did. He sent His Only-Begotten Son to earth that we might have life through Him. Saint Paul explains this plan of salvation saying:

> For when we were still without strength, in due time Christ died for the ungodly. For scarcely for a righteous man will one die; yet perhaps for a good man someone would even dare to die. But God demonstrates His own love toward us, in that while we were still sinners, Christ died for us. Much more then, having now been justified by His blood, we shall be saved from wrath through Him. For if when we were enemies we were reconciled to God through the death of His Son, much more, having been reconciled, we shall be saved by His life. And not only *that*, but we also rejoice in God through our Lord Jesus Christ, through whom we have now received the reconciliation. Therefore, just as through one man sin entered the world, and death through sin, and thus death spread to all men, because all sinned—(For until the law sin was in the world, but sin is not imputed when there is no law. Nevertheless death reigned from Adam to Moses, even over those who had not sinned according to the likeness of the transgression of Adam, who is a type of Him who was to come. But the free gift is not like the offense. For if by the one man's offense many died, much more the grace of God and the gift by the grace of the one Man, Jesus Christ, abounded to many. And the gift *is* not like *that which came* through the one who sinned. For the judgment *which came* from one *offense resulted* in condemnation, but the free gift which came from many offenses *resulted* in justification. For if by the one man's offense death reigned through the one, much more those who receive abundance of grace and of the gift of righteousness will reign in life through the One, Jesus Christ.) Therefore, as through one man's offense *judgment* came to all men, resulting in condemnation, even so through one Man's righteous act *the free gift came* to all men, resulting in justification of life. For as by

> one man's disobedience many were made sinners, so also by one Man's obedience many will be made righteous. Moreover the law entered that the offense might abound. But where sin abounded, grace abounded much more, so that as sin reigned in death, even so grace might reign through righteousness to eternal life through Jesus Christ our Lord.[12]

In order for the Redeemer to be able to redeem humanity He is required to have these qualities: 1) He must be fully human, for it was man who fell, and so the Redeemer would represent the human race in receiving punishment for the transgression. 2) He must die, for God's penalty for Adam and Eve was death: "You shall die,"[13] and also because "The wages of sin is death."[14] 3) He must be infinite, so that He can repay our infinite debt. As sin was directed against the infinite God, all humanity had a share in this debt. 4) He must be without sin, for how could He redeem us if He Himself is a sinner, in need of redemption? 5) He must be a creator, for His role is not confined to forgiveness alone, but is extended to regenerating human nature by the Holy Spirit.

Therefore, when the Hypostasis of the Word, the Logos, the Divine Wisdom, took flesh and lived among us, He became capable of redeeming us; fulfilling all of the requirements for redemption. By His humanity, He is a Man subject to death. By His Divinity, He is the infinite, sinless Creator. So from all of the above, we can see that the Word's Incarnation was part of the Divine economy since the beginning of time — the Lord Jesus Christ's Divinity *is eternal.* He is always Divine, and was not made Divine by the Emperor Constantine. I must also again emphasize that the coming to earth of the Lord Jesus Christ was for a fundamental purpose. This purpose was not to "solidify Constantine's power base" or to assist members of the early Church to "expand their own power;" but it was part of God's Divine plan of salvation for the entire human race. It is utterly preposterous for Dan Brown to assert that Jesus Christ was a mere man who became a deity overnight, for this entirely debases the

---

[12] Rom. 5:6–21.

[13] Gen. 2:17

[14] Rom. 6:23.

plan of God and dismisses the true purpose of the manifestation of God the Son in the flesh. As Saint Cyril of Alexandria, the Pillar of Orthodoxy, states, "In the person of Christ, a man has not become God; God has become man."

Affirmations of the existence of the second Hypostasis (Person) of the Holy Trinity are strongly substantiated in both the Old and New Testaments of the Holy Bible, which, as we have already noted, existed in its entirety before the Council of Nicaea. In Genesis, the Son Himself spoke to Adam in the Garden of Eden. Saint Theophilus of Antioch (115–181 A.D.) explains this saying:

> The God and Father, indeed, of all cannot be contained … But His Word, through whom He made all things, being His power and His wisdom … went to the garden in the person of God, and conversed with Adam. For the divine writing itself teaches us that Adam said that he heard the voice. But what else is this voice but the Word of God, who is also His Son?[15]

In actual fact, the Son Himself also appeared again in the Old Testament to Hagar the bondwoman,[16] Abraham the Patriarch,[17] our father Jacob,[18] Moses the Archprophet,[19] the prophet Balaam,[20] to Gideon,[21] and to Manoah and his wife[22] as the *Angel of the Lord*. All of the appearances of the Angel of the Lord in the Old Testament are manifestations of the second Person of the Holy Trinity—that is, Christ the Logos—thousands of years before His Incarnation in human form. Saint Cyprian (ca. 200–258 A.D.) confirms this for us saying:

> Christ also is Himself the Word of God…the same is Angel and God. That Christ is God… Christ is at once Angel and God. In Genesis to Abraham: "And the Angel of the Lord called him from

[15] Saint Theophilus, *Theophilus to Autolycus, ANF*, 2.103.
[16] Gen. 16:7–13.
[17] Gen. 18:1–3; 22:1–18.
[18] Gen. 32:24–30.
[19] Ex. 3:1–4:17.
[20] Num. 22:22–35.
[21] Jud. 6:12–22.
[22] Jud. 13:3–22.

> heaven and said to him, Abraham! Abraham! And he said, Here am I. And He said, Lay not your hand upon the lad, neither do anything to him. For now I know that you fear your God, and have not spared your son, your beloved son, for My sake (Gen. 22:11–12).[23]

Saint Irenaeus (ca. 140–202 A.D.) elucidates the same when he writes:

> Again Moses says that the Son of God drew near to exchange speech with Abraham: *and God appeared to him at the oak of Mambre at midday, and lifting up his eyes, he saw, and behold, three men were standing over him; and he prostrated himself to the ground and said: Lord, if I have truly found favour before thee* (Gen. 18:1–3); and all the rest of his speech is with the Lord, and the Lord speaks to him. Two, then, of the three were angels, but one the Son of God; and with Him Abraham also spoke ... So Abraham was a prophet, and saw what was to come to pass in the future, the Son of God in human form ... Jacob also, while journeying into Mesopotamia, sees Him, in a dream, standing at the ladder, that is the Cross ... set up from earth even to heaven (Gen. 28:12–15) ... And all visions of this kind signify the Son of God, in His speaking with men and being with them; for it is not the Father of all, who is not seen by the world, the Creator of all who said: *Heaven is my throne, and the earth my footstool; what manner of house will you build for me, or what is the place of my rest?* (Is. 66.1 quoted in Acts 7.49) and who *holds the land in His fist and the heavens in His span* (Isa. 40.12) — it is not He who would stand circumscribed in space and speak with Abraham, but the Word of God, who was always with mankind, and foretold what was to come to pass in the future, and acquainted man with God.[24]

Saint Justin Martyr (ca. 110–165 A.D.) also calls the Son "both Angel, and God" and explains that "God distinct from the Father conversed with Moses." He says, "this same One alone who is called an Angel, and who is God, appeared to and communed with Moses."[25] Having

[23] Saint Cyprian, *Treatise XII: Second Book: Testimonies*, *ANF*, 5.515, 517.
[24] Saint Irenaeus, *Proofs of the Apostolic Preaching*, *Ancient Christian Writers*, 16.76–7.
[25] Saint Justin Martyr, *Dialogue with Trypho*, *ANF*, 1.227.

spoken with the Son Himself, who is God, Hagar "called the name of the LORD who spoke to her"[26] explicitly declaring His Divinity saying: "You-Are-the-God-Who-Sees... Have I also here seen Him who sees me?"[27] The Book of Judges also tells us that after seeing Christ "Manoah knew that He was the Angel of the LORD" and so Manoah and his wife proclaimed: "We shall surely die, because we have seen God!"[28] So this very same Person—who appeared as the Angel of the Lord in the Old Testament—is the very same Person who was incarnate, took flesh, and became Man. This very same Person is the Second Hypostasis, who is the Son of God, who is Jesus Christ the Word incarnate in the fullness of time, who *is* God. The writings of the early Church Fathers and authors (before and after Nicaea) contain many more references to the Angel of the Lord as "Christ," "the Son of God," "God," and "Jesus" but of course, it is not possible to include all of these here. The Old Testament, in addition, contains many prophecies concerning the Incarnation of Jesus Christ, as well as prophecies concerning the Virgin birth. When we say that Saint Mary, the ever-virgin, is the Birthgiver of God, we are confirming the Divinity of her Son, Jesus Christ. The Son of God became the Son of Man—the Word incarnate. That is why when we confirm that Saint Mary is the Birthgiver of God, we are confirming a certain truth about Jesus Christ.

During His time on earth as a Man, the Lord Jesus Christ Himself testified numerous times that He is God and His words are recorded in the New Testament. Saint Mark the Evangelist, who was an eyewitness of the Lord's Crucifixion, Resurrection, and Ascension, gives the following account of the trial of Jesus in his gospel which was written between 55 and 65 A.D.:[29] "But He kept silent and answered nothing. Again the high priest asked Him, "Are you the Christ, the Son of the

---

[26] Gen. 16:11.

[27] Gen. 16:13.

[28] Jud. 13:21–22.

[29] Because of Saint Mark's inclusion of Jesus Christ's prophecy concerning the destruction of the Temple in 13:2, we can be certain that Saint Mark's gospel was written before 70 A.D.

Blessed?" And Jesus said, "I am. And you will see the Son of Man sitting at the right hand of the Power, and coming with the clouds of heaven."[30] So Christians did not believe that Jesus Christ is the Son of God because the Emperor Constantine declared this to be so; but they have always believed that Jesus Christ is God because He Himself revealed His Divinity saying, "I and *My* Father are one."[31]

The New Testament writers (prior to Nicaea) fully recognized that the Lord Jesus Christ is God. One outstanding example, is Saint John the Apostle. Around one-hundred years after the Lord Jesus Christ's Crucifixion, Resurrection, and Ascension into heaven, Saint John the Apostle wrote his gospel. It was authored after he wrote the Book of Revelation and his other epistles; and long after the three evangelists Saints Matthew, Mark, and Luke had written their gospels. Saint John wrote his gospel specifically to elucidate beyond any doubt, the Divinity and Person of Jesus Christ. The events and miracles performed by Jesus Christ in Saint John's gospel, as well as the many proclamations of the Son's eternal communion with the Father, manifestly declare the Omnipotent, Omnipresent God: the Creator, the incarnate Logos. As Saint John says: All things were made through Him " [Jesus Christ], and without Him nothing was made that was made."[32] Extant copies of the original manuscript of Saint John's Gospel have been preserved, and this again proves without a doubt that long before the Council of Nicaea, the Church believed that Jesus Christ is Divine.

Furthermore, Saint Paul in his Epistle to the Colossians writes specifically of Christ saying: "He is the image of the invisible God, the firstborn over all creation. For by Him all things were created that are in heaven and that are on earth, visible and invisible, whether thrones or dominions or principalities or powers. All things were created through Him and for Him. And He is before all things, and in Him all things consist."[33] Saint Paul, by the inspiration of the Holy Spirit, wrote these

[30] Mk. 14:61–2.
[31] Jn. 10:30.
[32] Jn. 1:3.
[33] Col. 1:16–17.

verses based on the Old Testament's many proclamations that God is the Creator. So there is no question that Saint Paul was affirming the absolute and eternal Divinity of Jesus Christ.

With regards to Dan Brown's claim that "Thousands of documents already existed chronicling [Jesus'] life as a mortal man," as I explained in the previous chapter these were heretical writings, strongly and rightly rejected by the Church. It is also important to note that these documents most certainly were not numbered in the "thousands." In contrast, the Ante-Nicene Fathers, who received the *true* doctrines concerning the Lord Jesus Christ directly from the Holy Apostles, articulated the *correct* belief in the Holy Trinity and in the Divinity of Christ. The following examples from the writings of the Church Fathers and early Christian authors, each were written before the Council of Nicaea, once again highlighting Dan Brown's lie that before a vote at the council Jesus Christ "was viewed by His followers as a mortal prophet." The writings all confirm Christ's deity:

> **Saint Ignatius of Antioch, ca. 115 A.D:**
> Do not be led astray by strange doctrines and ancient unprofitable myths... For the divinely inspired prophets lived in expectation of Jesus Christ: and therefore they were persecuted, being inspired by His grace so that unbelievers might be convinced that there is one God who has displayed Himself through Jesus Christ His Son, who is His Word... who in all respects was pleasing to him who sent Him.[34]

> **Bishop Melito of Sardis, ca. 170 A.D:**
> This Being is perfect Reason, the Word of God; He who was begotten before the light; He who is Creator together with the Father; He who is the Fashioner of men; He who is all in all; He who among the patriarchs is Patriarch; He who in the law is the Law; among the priests, Chief Priests; among kings, the Ruler... in the Father, the Son; in God, God... He who is seated at the right hand of the Father... the recoverer of those that are lost; the light of those that are in darkness... the guide of those that go astray... the bride-

[34] Saint Ignatius, *To the Ephesians, in Bettenson. The Early Christian Fathers*, 58.

groom of the Church; the charioteer of the cherubim ... God who is from God; the Son who is from the Father; Jesus Christ the King forevermore. Amen.[35]

Saint Irenaeus, ca. 182–188 A.D:

For I have shown from the Scriptures, that no one of the sons of Adam is as to everything, and absolutely, called God, or named Lord. But that He is Himself in His own right, beyond all men who ever lived, God, and Lord, and King Eternal, and the incarnate Word, proclaimed by all the prophets, the apostles, and by the Spirit Himself, may be seen by all who have attained to even a small portion of the truth. Now, the Scriptures would not have testified these things of Him, if, like others, He had been a mere man.[36]

Saint Cyprian, ca. 250 A.D:

Christ is God ... In Isaiah: ... "God is in You and there is no other God beside You. For You are God, and we knew it not, O God of Israel, our Savior" (Is. 45:14–15) ... Moreover, in Jeremiah: "This is our God, and no other shall be esteemed beside Him, who has found all the way of knowledge and has given it to Jacob His son and to Israel, His beloved. After this, He was seen upon earth, and He conversed with men" (Bar. 3:35–37) ... Also in the Gospel according to John: "In the beginning was the Word, and the Word was with God and the Word was God." (Jn. 1:1) Also in the same: "The Lord said to Thomas, reach your finger here, and look at My hands ... Do not be unbelieving but believing. Thomas answered and said unto him, "My Lord and my God." (Jn. 20: 27–8) ... Also, Saint Paul to the Romans: "... Christ came, who is God over all, blessed for evermore." (Rom. 9:3-5). Also, in the Apocalypse: "I am the Alpha and Omega, the beginning and the end ... He that overcomes will possess these things and their inheritance; and I will be his God and he will be My son." (Rev. 21: 6, 7) ... Also in the Gospel according to Saint Matthew: "And you will call His name Emmanuel, which is, being interpreted, 'God with us.'" (Matt. 1:23).[37]

---

[35] Bishop Melito of Sardis, *On Faith*, *ANF* 8.756–7.

[36] Saint Irenaeus, *Against Heresies*.

[37] Saint Cyprian, *Treatise XII: Second Book: Testimonies*, *ANF*, 5.517–18.

> **Saint Athanasius the Apostolic, 318 A.D:**
> While God, the Word Himself, Who was united with the body, while ordering all things, also by the works He did in the body showed Himself to be not man, but God the Word... Who that saw Him healing the diseases to which the human race is subject, can still think Him man and not God?... For who that saw Him give back what was deficient to men born lacking, and open the eyes of the man blind from his birth, would have failed to perceive that the nature of men was subject to Him, and that He was its Artificer and Maker? Therefore, even to begin with, when He was descending to us, He fashioned His body for Himself from a Virgin, thus to afford to all no small proof of His Godhead, in that He Who formed this is also Maker of everything else as well... For who that saw His power over evil spirits, or who that saw the evil spirits confess that He was their Lord, will hold his mind any longer in doubt whether this be the Son and Wisdom and Power of God? For He made even the creation break silence: in that even at His death, marvellous to relate, or rather at his actual trophy over death—the Cross I mean—all creation was confessing that He that was made manifest and suffered in the body was not merely man, but the Son of God and Saviour of all... For the sun hid his face, and the earth quaked and the mountains were rent; and all men were awed. Now these things showed that Christ on the cross was God, while all creation was His slave, and was witnessing by its fear to its Master's presence.[38]

Other Church Fathers and Christian authors who also wrote, prior to Nicaea, that the Lord Jesus Christ is God incarnate, include: Saint Dionysius, fourteenth Pope of Alexandria; Saint Alexander, nineteenth Pope of Alexandria; Clement of Alexandria; Tertullian; and Saint Justin Martyr, to name a few.

Concerning the Council of Nicaea, Dan Brown again deceives his readers. The council was not convened to vote upon the Divinity of Jesus Christ. Rather, the gathering was held to deal with the Arian heresy. Earlier, in the year 318 A.D., Pope Alexander of Alexandria summoned nearly one hundred Egyptian hierarchies to a synod in which

---

[38] Saint Athanasius, *On the Incarnation*, *NPNF: Second Series*, 4.45–46.

Arius—a priest from Alexandria—was condemned, and he and his adherents deposed. Later at the Council of Nicaea, Pope Alexander's sentence was not only sustained but confirmed. It was at this council that the famous Nicene Creed was written. This Creed was primarily formulated by Saint Athanasius the Apostolic, and agreed upon by the council in response to the controversial teaching of Arius.[39] The teachings of Arius threatened to tear apart the Christian Empire ruled, at that time, by the Emperor Constantine the Great. Brown's statement that Emperor Constantine convened the ecumenical council to "strengthen the new Christian tradition" by establishing the Divinity of Jesus Christ is entirely false. In reality, he convened the council to avoid damage to the already established upright Christian faith and true Orthodox doctrines of the Church. At the end of the Council of Nicaea, a vote by 316 bishops of the 318 in attendance, resolved that Arius be excommunicated as a heretic, and that his teachings pronounced heretical. So the vote was not a vote to decide on Jesus' Divinity, and neither was it a close vote as Brown would have us believe.

The core of Arius' teaching was that he considered the Son as the first creation by nature subject to change, and that He was subject to sin along with the rest of creation. Arius proclaimed that since the Son is "born" and that the Father is the only "unborn," then the Father alone is God because He is superior to the Son. He further declared that since the Son is born, there is a beginning to His existence and "there was a time when He was not;" therefore claiming that the Son's origin was out of nothing. According to Arius, God was not always Father, and there was a time when He was not a Father. He also claimed that the Son is not of the same essence as the Father but a stranger to the Divine essence of the Father, and therefore different from it.

The Holy Coptic Orthodox Church in Her efforts in bridging the gap between churches, has, during the papacy of His Holiness Pope Shenouda III (1972–present) held Christological dialogues with the

[39] This upright proclamation of the true Christian faith is, to this day, recited daily by all Orthodox Christians.

Eastern Orthodox Churches or Chalcedonian Churches, the Roman Catholic Church, the Anglican Church, and the Reformed Churches in the Netherlands. Together we have signed an Agreed Statement on Christology. The Christological Statement is based on the following framework; and although the phraseology may differ from church to church, the belief is consistent:

> "We believe that our Lord, God and Savior Jesus Christ, the incarnate — Logos is perfect in His Divinity and perfect in His humanity. He made His humanity One with His Divinity without Mixture, nor Mingling, nor Confusion. His Divinity was not separated from His humanity even for a moment or a twinkling of an eye..."[40]

This means that Jesus Christ is *eternally* Divine, and the entire Christian Church has, and always will, expressly proclaim that "Jesus Christ our Lord is God."

In response to Brown's statement that many aspects of Christianity were debated and voted upon at the Council of Nicaea, including the date of Easter, the role of the bishops, and the administration of sacraments (*DVC*, 253), following is a brief summary of the canons — or laws — of the council. After the rejection of the Arian heresy and the writing of the Nicene Creed with its anathemas, "the bishops turned to matters of church discipline and drew up twenty canons dealing with actual problems affecting the orderly administration of ecclesiastical affairs."[41] A number of canons (including the fourth, seventh, and fifteenth canons) involved matters concerning the organizational structure of the church, and of jurisdiction relating to the sees of Alexandria, Antioch, and Jerusalem. Six other canons dealt with issues relating to the clergy. Four canons addressed the topic of reconciliation of those who had lapsed during recent persecutions and outlined guidelines for repentance and readmission to the Holy Eucharist. Two canons dealt

---

[40] From the *Agreed Statement on Christology* between the Coptic Orthodox Church and the Roman Catholic Church, at the Monastery of Saint Bishoy in Egypt, 12 February, 1988

[41] Davis, *The First Seven Ecumenical Councils (325–787): Their History and Theology*, 63.

with the readmission to the Church of schismatics and heretics such as the Novatianists and the followers of Paul of Samosata. In another canon the council addressed the role of deacons and prescribed standing during prayer; and finally, in the last canon, the bishops agreed that the Feast of the Resurrection should be celebrated at the same time throughout the Empire.[42]

Yet again, it is clear that Brown's facts are not correct. For example, there was no discussion at the Council of Nicaea about the administration of the sacraments, rather a discussion about readmission for the lapsed into *one* sacrament; there was no discussion about the role of bishops but about the *jurisdiction* of bishops. Thus, concerning Brown's claims about what was debated upon at the council, his so-called facts appear to be close to the truth, but they are not accurate.

---

[42] Ibid., 68.

CHAPTER EIGHT

Mary Magdalene, the Church, and the Goddess

Brown's treatment of Mary Magdalene is sheer delusion.

Sandra Miesel (Crisis Magazine)[1]

1. Dan's Deceptions about the Lord Jesus Christ and Mary Magdalene

- Mary Magdalene was Jesus' wife (*DVC*: the Movie).
- One particularly troubling earthly theme kept recurring in the gospels. Mary Magdalene... More specifically her marriage to Jesus Christ (*DVC*, 264).
- The marriage of Jesus and Mary Magdalene is part of the historical record (*DVC*, 265).
- The legend of the Holy Grail is a legend about royal blood. When Grail legend speaks of 'the chalice that held the blood of Christ'... it speaks, in fact, of Mary Magdalene—the female womb that carried Jesus' royal bloodline (*DVC*, 270).
- Mary Magdalene was the Holy Vessel. She was the chalice that bore the lineage, and the vine from which the sacred fruit sprang forth! (*DVC*, 270).

The Truth about the Lord Jesus Christ and Mary Magdalene

In Chapter Three, we noted that Dan Brown maintains Mary Magdalene was of the House of Benjamin, and therefore she was of royal

[1] Miesel, "Dismantling *The Da Vinci Code*."

descent; that Jesus — a mere mortal — was of the House of David, a descendent of King Solomon, and therefore King of the Jews; and that the marriage of Jesus and Mary Magdalene — a fusion of two royal bloodlines — created a potent political union with the potential of making a legitimate claim to the throne and restoring the line of kings as it was under Solomon (*DVC*, 270). At the end of *The Da Vinci Code*, we are told that Sophie Neveu and her brother are the last living descendants of Jesus Christ. In responding to these ideas, as well as to the falsehoods mentioned above, we must consider what Brown has said about a marriage between Jesus Christ and Mary Magdalene logically.

We must not forget that Brown states Jesus Christ is a "mortal man" who is not Divine.[2] We must also remember that Brown asserts Mary Magdalene is the sacred feminine and that she is of the Tribe of Benjamin. Based on this information, it would be fair to conclude that Brown would have us believe the following: Mary Magdalene — a goddess from the Tribe of Benjamin, married Jesus — an ordinary mortal man from the Tribe of Judah; together they had children, and their bloodline survives to the present day. This begs the fundamental question: If Jesus Christ Who, according to Brown, is not the Son of God and Who is not Divine, fathered children by a divine Mary Magdalene why would His alleged bloodline be of any importance? This idea also leads me to ask: Why would a goddess be interested in an ordinary man, what purpose could he serve her, and why would she be in need of him? Dan Brown has sparked a worldwide controversy of enormous magnitude about the descendants of Jesus Christ; but if as Brown supposes, Christ is not Divine His alleged descendants, then, should be thought of as having no significance in modern society. As earlier discussed, the Christian Church has always affirmed that Jesus Christ is God, and that Mary Magdalene is a mortal woman; not a goddess.

It is also necessary to point out that the Israelites married from within their own tribes; so a person from the Tribe of Judah would not marry

[2] What is perhaps most interesting is that while he claims that Jesus is not Divine, Brown insists on keeping the capital H for the word "His" throughout *The Da Vinci Code*.

a person from the Tribe of Benjamin. But supposing we accepted Dan Brown's theory that this is not an impossibility? We are then led us to ask: Why does Brown not consider the marriage of any woman from the Tribe of Benjamin to any man from the Tribe of Judah to be as special as that of the alleged marriage between Jesus Christ and Mary Magdalene? Logically, if what Brown is claiming is fact, then a marriage between two people from the Tribes of Benjamin and Judah would also be a "fusion of the two royal bloodlines." Which presses one to ask yet another question: Why is the union of Jesus and Mary Magdalene seen by Brown as the most important? And on what basis does Brown agree that Jesus is the King of the Jews? If he believes that Jesus is the King of the Jews based on Biblical prophecies and the New Testament accounts, why then does he brush aside the fact that the Bible explicitly declares the Divinity of Jesus Christ? Some of Brown's sources—*The Templar Revelation* in particular—assert that during the sexual union of Mary Magdalene and Jesus, her divinity, her royal blood, and her passing on of gnosis to Him, made Jesus King. Of course, the Holy Orthodox Church outrightly rejects all such nonsense.

Having said all of this, I must again emphasize that Dan Brown has founded his entire royal bloodline theory on fabrications that are contradictory, and that do not make sense. With reference to the Tribes of Judah and Benjamin, the Tribe of Benjamin is not a "royal" tribe. In addition, the prophecies of the Old Testament, and their fulfillment in the New Testament, declare that the King and Messiah came only and specifically from the Tribe of Judah. So the Tribe of Judah, or the House of David, is the only Tribe which can claim a "royal" dynasty because it is the tribe from which the Lord Jesus Christ, God incarnate descended. Furthermore, there is no Biblical, historical, or empirical evidence to support the claim that Mary Magdalene was of the Tribe of Benjamin. And so, when we combine this information with the details of the truth about the Priory of Sion and the Knights Templar previously discussed, we can clearly see that there is no such thing as the royal bloodline of Jesus Christ.

The above discussion notwithstanding, the Holy Orthodox Church strongly affirms that the Lord Jesus Christ was never married, was never involved in any sexual union, and never fathered children. Like *The Templar Revelation* that has Jesus and Mary Magdalene as unmarried sexual partners in a sacred marriage, one of Brown's other sources—*The Woman with the Alabaster Jar*—uses ancient goddess rites and anointing ceremonies to also conclude that Jesus and Mary Magdalene were united in a sacred marriage. But as I outlined, in Chapter Six, Jesus Christ did not have a carnal relationship with Mary Magdalene, for such an act would undermine God's Divine plan to redeem humanity. But the real issue here is not what one thinks of such ideas, since they are all utterly gratuitous assertions and ones which are vehemently rejected by the Holy Orthodox Church. However, the issue is one of evidence. Brown states that the marriage of Jesus and Mary Magdalene is "part of the historical record" and that "if Jesus were not married, at least one of the Bible's gospels would have mentioned it" (*DVC*, 265). But actually it is quite the opposite—what evidence, Biblical, historical, or other has proven that Jesus Christ was ever married? The answer is none. There is not a single text in the entire Holy Bible, in early Christian records, or in any writings of the early Church Fathers confirming a marriage between Jesus Christ and Mary Magdalene. Even the Gnostic gospels, from which Brown draws information, do not make any claims about Jesus Christ as a married man, or His involvement in any type of sexual relationship.

The four Gospels, which are the most accurate sources for details about the life of Jesus Christ, portray Mary Magdalene as one His important followers. And as such, there are numerous references to Mary Magdalene in the true Gospels:

- She is described as the woman from whom the Lord Jesus Christ cast out seven demons (Mk. 16:9; Lk. 8:2).
- She is one of the women who accompanied the Lord Jesus Christ in His ministry (Lk. 8:2).
- She witnessed the crucifixion and death of the Lord (Matt. 27:56; Mk. 15:40; Lk. 23:46-49, Jn. 19:25).
- She was present at the Lord's burial (Matt. 27:61; Mk. 15:47, Lk. 23:55).

- She witnessed the Lord's empty tomb (Matt. 28:1–10; Mk. 16:1–8; Lk. 24:1–10); and
- After His Resurrection, the Lord Jesus Christ appeared to her alone at the tomb (Mk. 16:9; Jn. 20:1–18).

So the Gospels make clear the fact that Mary Magdalene was a follower of Jesus, but not once do they provide even the slightest indication that Mary Magdalene, or any other woman, was His spouse. In point of fact, the Gospels also do not indicate that Mary Magdalene herself was ever married. She is mentioned with "Mary the mother of James and Joses, and the mother of Zebedee's sons,"[3] "Joanna the wife of Chuza,"[4] and with the names of other women, such as Jesus' "mother" and "Mary the wife of Clopas."[5] What is evident here is that Mary Magdalene is often identified with her hometown of Magdala,[6] but she is never identified with a man, or mentioned as "the wife of" any man. These Gospel accounts, therefore, once again confirm that Mary Magdalene was not married to Jesus Christ.

Furthermore, the Holy Orthodox Church has *never* referred to, or believed that, Mary Magdalene is the Holy Grail or the Chalice that carried the blood of Jesus Christ. The "female womb that carried Jesus' royal bloodline" to which Brown so often refers, is discarded by the Holy Orthodox Church as pure fantasy for the reasons we have mentioned. For Brown to say that "Mary Magdalene was the Holy Vessel…the chalice that bore the lineage, and the vine from which the sacred fruit sprang forth" is incorrect in its entirety. Here Brown takes the epithet "the vine," which is an epithet of the Holy Mother God used to honour her and glorify her Son Jesus Christ, and falsely and blasphemously applies it to Mary Magdalene. At the beginning of the Divine Liturgy of Saint Basil the Great, we chant: "Hail to Mary the Queen, the unaged vine that no farmer toiled. In her was found the Cluster of Life. Truly the Son of God took flesh from the Virgin. She gave birth to Him; He

---

[3] Matt. 27:56.

[4] Lk. 8:3.

[5] Jn. 19:25.

[6] A town on the western shore of the Sea of Galilee.

saved us and forgave us our sins."[7] The Cluster of Life referred to here is Jesus Christ—the Word, the Son of God, Who took flesh from the Holy Virgin Saint Mary and dwelt in her womb for nine full months. So we can say that *Jesus Christ* is the sacred fruit which sprang forth from the Virgin Saint Mary; but we cannot say that Mary Magdalene is the vine, and we wholly reject Brown's naming of her alleged descendants "the sacred fruit" for this term is reserved specifically for Jesus Christ. In the Holy Orthodox Church, we constantly praise the Ever-Virgin Saint Mary with her kinswoman Elizabeth proclaiming: "Blessed *are* you among women, and blessed is the fruit of your womb!"[8] Therefore, the Holy Bible itself affirms that "the fruit" that was in the womb of Saint Mary is the Lord Jesus Christ.

With regards to Mary Magdalene as the "Holy Vessel" the Holy Orthodox rejects the use of this term to describe her because she did *not* carry the blood of Christ. The only woman who can be referred to as the Holy Grail is the Holy Virgin Saint Mary. As the true chalice, she carried the blood of the Lord Jesus Christ, because He dwelt in her womb for nine full months. The true chalice or the "Holy Vessel" which carries the blood of Jesus Christ—shed for the salvation of the whole world—is also the Cup that we daily behold on the altar in the Holy Eucharist. So the Holy Grail is *not* Mary Magdalene. These are the only explanations of the phrase "the chalice that held the blood of Christ" that the Holy Orthodox Church accepts. A depiction of these interpretations also features predominantly in icons in the Russian Orthodox and Greek Orthodox traditions (plates 3 and 4). These icons confirm that the Holy Virgin carried the blood of Christ—namely, the Word Himself—in her womb; and that the Cup of the Holy Eucharist that holds the blood of Jesus Christ is the Cup which is ever-flowing.

[7] Excerpt of a hymn chanted at the start of the Divine Liturgy as the priest/s and deacons dress in their tunics. It is also chanted during the existing procession as part of the Coptic wedding rite (cf. *The Three Coptic Divine Liturgies: Diocese of Sydney and Affiliated Regions: Study Version*, 274).
[8] Lk. 1:42

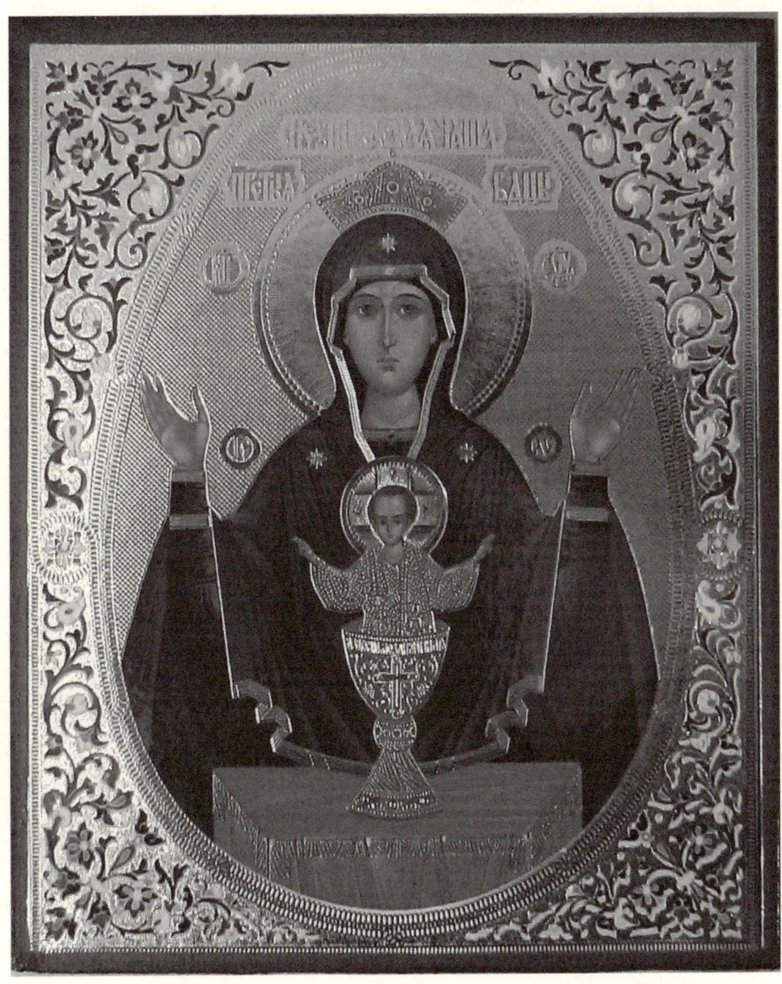

PLATE 3. Russian and Greek Orthodox icon of the Holy Mother of God and the Lord Jesus Christ (Metropolitan Bishoy, Private Collection). The words "The Ever-Flowing Cup" are inscribed at the top. The second and third lines of inscription read "The Mother of God" in Russian and Greek respectively; followed by the words "Jesus Christ" in Greek.

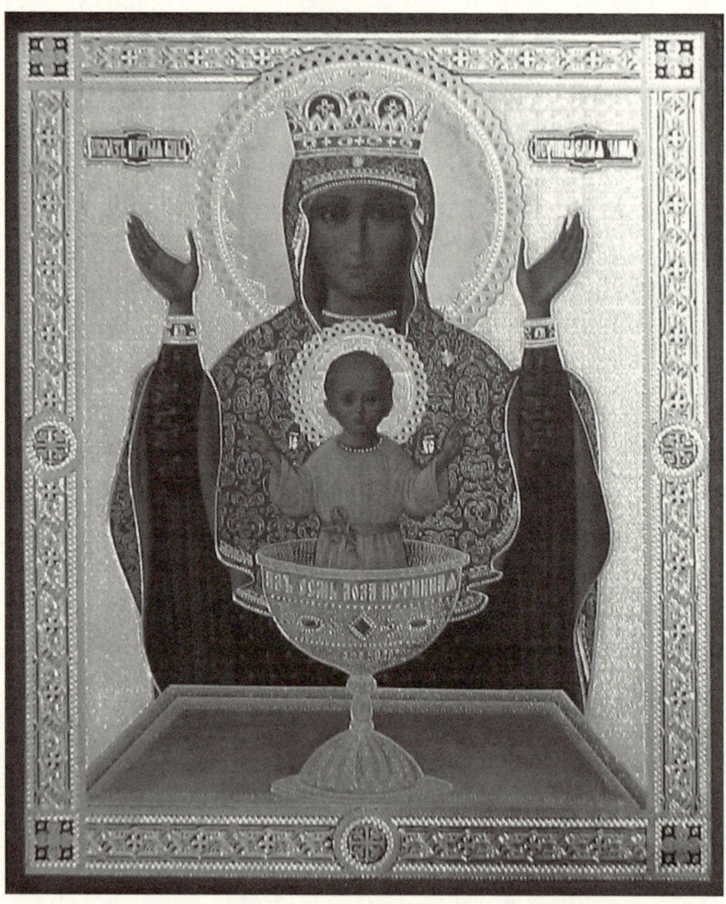

PLATE 4. Russian Orthodox icon of the Holy Mother of God and the Lord Jesus Christ (Metropolitan Bishoy, Private Collection).

Jesus Christ, the Word incarnate, proclaims the nearness of the Kingdom of God, and many times He challenges those who would follow Him to abandon their possessions or leave their families for His sake. So it is clear that Jesus was not personally preoccupied with domestic family life. The Lord Jesus Christ also emphasized that His Kingdom "is not of this world,"[9] thus confirming His primary concern for His heavenly and eternal Kingdom. As God incarnate, Jesus Christ did not seek to establish an earthly kingdom or a royal bloodline. Therefore, the Holy Orthodox Church refutes any claims that the Lord Jesus Christ was either married or involved in any sexual union.

2. Dan's Deceptions about Leonardo and The Last Supper

- Da Vinci had always been an awkward subject for historians, especially in the Christian tradition. Despite the visionary's genius, he was a flamboyant homosexual and worshipper of Nature's divine order, both of which place him in a perpetual state of sin against God... Even Da Vinci's enormous output of breathtaking Christian art only furthered the artist's reputation for spiritual hypocrisy. Accepting hundreds of lucrative Vatican commissions, Da Vinci painted Christian themes not as an expression of his own beliefs but rather as a commercial venture—a means of funding a lavish lifestyle (*DVC*, 50).
- Sophie looked down at the painting, seeing to her astonishment that everyone at the table had a glass of wine, including Christ... There was no chalice in the painting. No Holy Grail... A bit strange... considering that both the Bible and our standard Grail legend celebrate this moment as the definitive arrival of the Holy Grail. Oddly Da Vinci appears to have forgotten to paint the cup of Christ (*DVC*, 256).
- *The Last Supper* practically shouts at the viewer that Jesus and Magdalene were a pair (*DVC*, 264).

[9] Jn. 18:36.

- The [individual] seated in the place of honour, at the right hand of the Lord ... had flowing red hair, delicate folded hands, and the hint of a bosom. It was without a doubt ... female (*DVC*, 263).
- The woman to Jesus' right was young and pious-looking, with a demure face, beautiful red hair, and hands folded quietly ... That ... is Mary Magdalene (*DVC*, 263).

Brown further attests that the presence of a "V" shape (symbolic of the chalice and a female womb) and an "M" shape (representing Mary Magdalene) in the painting is evidence that the figure to Jesus' right is Mary Magdalene and not Saint John (*DVC*, 265).

- In the painting, Peter was leaning menacingly toward Mary Magdalene and slicing his blade-like hand across her neck (*DVC*, 269).

Brown also claims that near Saint Peter is a disembodied hand wielding a dagger (*DVC*, 269).

The Truth about Leonardo and The Last Supper

Bruce Boucher—Curator of European Decorative Arts and Sculpture at the Art Institute of Chicago—points out in a *New York Times* article[10] that most of Dan Brown claims about Leonardo are incorrect and that his grasp of the historical Leonardo is shaky: "One small but telling point comes in Mr. Brown's references to Leonardo as "Da Vinci," as if that were the painter's last name, yet it is no surname but simply a reference to the fact that he was the ... son of Ser Piero of Vinci, in the Florentine territory. Like other great artists, with or without last names, Leonardo is invariably referred to by his given name and not by da Vinci." Boucher further explains that although there was one alleged incident of homosexuality early in Leonardo's adulthood, the evidence of his sexual orientation remains inconclusive and fragmentary. Brown's exaggeration in calling Leonardo a "flamboyant homosexual" is inaccurate, and moreover, Leonardo did not worship the divine order of nature. On the point of Leonardo's "enormous output" of Christian art and "hundreds

[10] Boucher, "Does The Da Vinci Code Crack Leonardo?"

of lucrative Vatican commissions," he was, in fact, infamous for his very meager production of artwork; and by most accounts, he received one commission from the Vatican and spent little time in Rome.[11]

In *The Da Vinci Code*, Dan Brown cites the famous painting, *The Last Supper*, by Leonardo in an attempt to substantiate his claim that Jesus Christ and Mary Magdalene were married. Nearly all of his false interpretations of this famous work come directly from pages 22–25 of *The Templar Revelation*. First of all Brown contradicts himself by telling us the "fresco portrayed Jesus and His disciples at the moment Jesus announced one of them would betray Him (*DVC*, 255), and then on the very next page he says that the painting depicts the moment of the arrival of the cup of Christ. Here Brown is only half correct, since *The Last Supper* does not depict the moment of the consecration of the Eucharist. Boucher states that the composition "conforms to traditional Florentine depictions of the Last Supper, stressing the betrayal and sacrifice of Christ rather than the institution of the Eucharist and the chalice."[12] Steve Kellmeyer also confirms:

> What Leonardo was portraying here was not the moment of consecration, it was the moment of betrayal when the apostles are proclaiming that they will never abandon or betray Jesus Christ. Judas, Peter, and John are grouped together because they show the three reactions to Christ: Judas betrays Christ and never returns, Peter abandons Christ but he does return, John is the only one who never abandons or betrays Jesus Christ.[13]

Noted art historians further agree that *The Last Supper* depicts Chapter 13:21–30 of the Gospel of Saint John, which details the start of Judas' of betrayal of Jesus Christ. The late Professor Sir E. H. Gombrich tells us that:

> We can infer that Leonardo was commissioned to paint... [*The Last Supper*] around 1494 for the refectory of the Dominican monastery of Santa Maria delle Grazie in Milan... and we know that it

[11] Ibid.

[12] Ibid.

[13] Kellmeyer, interview in *The Da Vinci Code Deception* DVD.

> was completed in 1498, some four years later… One thing we can be sure about: Leonardo, like any other artist in his situation, had two sources on which to rely, the traditions of his art and the text of the Gospels, which, naturally, also form part of this tradition. It is remarkable that of the four accounts in the Gospel, tradition had long favoured the one in St John, despite the fact that St John does not mention the institution of the Eucharist which we generally associate with the Last Supper. The reason for this preference on the part of the painters may perhaps be found in the vivid episode that describes the action and the postures of the participants which…also inspired Leonardo.[14]

Therefore, the painting specifically dramatizes Jesus with His disciples at the end of the Jewish Paschal meal, before Judas leaves the Paschal table to betray Him, and before the institution of the Eucharist itself. It is the moment where Jesus warns, "One of you will betray me."[15] Based on the Gospel accounts, the Holy Orthodox Church, resolutely upholds the teaching that Judas was not present at the Eucharist and that he did not partake of the Holy Communion; thus his presence in the painting is yet another indication that the Lord's Supper had not yet begun. Gombrich again authenticates this idea saying: "In the Gospels of St Matthew and of St Mark the institution of the Eucharist, the dispensing of bread and wine, follows after this scene… In St Luke the Eucharist comes before the prophecy of the betrayal, but it should be noted that in Leonardo's Last Supper there is no visual allusion to this central scene."[16]

Dan Brown claims that the absence of a single material chalice for the Holy Eucharist in the painting confirms that Mary Magdalene is the true chalice that carried the blood of Christ. However, based on the fact that *The Last Supper* portrays the end of the Paschal meal, it is expected that there would be thirteen cups of wine on the table. This would also

[14] Gombrich, "Papers Given on the Occasion of the Dedication of the Last Supper (after Leonardo)."

[15] Jn. 13:21.

[16] Gombrich, "Papers Given on the Occasion of the Dedication of the Last Supper (after Leonardo)."

explain why the table is laden with bread and dishes. If Brown had simply bothered to research Jewish Passover history, he would have learned that in Passover tradition, each person in attendance at the Passover meal had their own cup, and that four cups of wine were drunk by each person. It is the third cup of the Passover meal which Jesus declared to be His Blood. Biblical scholar Alfred Edersheim, who converted from Judaism to Christianity, explains:

> After the regular Paschal meal ... the Lord instituted His own Supper, for the first time using the Aphikomen[17] "when He had given thanks" (after meat) ... [as] His body, and the third cup, or "cup of blessing which we bless" (1 Corinthians 10:16) — being "the cup after supper" (Luke 22:20) — ... [as] His blood. "And when they had sung a hymn" (Psalms 115–118) "they went out to the Mount of Olives" (Matthew 26:30).[18]

So Jesus Christ, did in fact, pass around *one cup* — His cup — to His disciples from which they all drank, but we cannot say that this single cup looked different to the other cups at the supper. And actually, the rites of the Passover meal would clearly indicate that this was not the case. We also cannot assume that at the time of the Eucharist Jesus interrupted the Passover meal proceedings in order to present a large silver or gold chalice, as there is no evidence for the true appearance of the cup used by Jesus Christ at the Last Supper. However, I must again emphasize that despite its shape or appearance, only *one cup* at the last supper contained the Holy Blood of the Lord Jesus Christ; and that *The Last Supper* by Leonardo shows Jesus Christ with His disciples before this event took place.

As for Brown's theory that the person sitting next to Jesus is not Saint John the Apostle, but Mary Magdalene, this is a product of Brown's skewed imagination. The person to the right of Jesus, is indeed Saint John; and not one credible art historian has agreed with Brown's theory or stated otherwise. Saint John is portrayed as an effeminate youth—a usual characteristic of male youths in paintings in Leonardo's period — and he

[17] Meaning "after-dish" comprising of a piece of unleavened cake.

[18] Edersheim, *The Temple: Its Ministry and Services as They Were at the Time of Jesus Christ*, 162.

is painted to Jesus' right in accordance with the Gospel account by Saint John himself, in which he states that he "was leaning on Jesus' bosom"[19] during the Last Supper. It is well known that as part of Passover tradition, the Paschal meal was to be eaten in a recumbent position "because it is the manner of slaves to eat standing, therefore now they eat sitting and leaning, in order to show they have been delivered from bondage into freedom."[20] But Professor Gombrich explains that:

> Tradition still had St John leaning against Christ, and the only rapid sketch we have by Leonardo for this composition indicates that he originally meant to adopt this tradition as well as the action of Christ reaching across the table to give the sop to Judas, who was generally placed there in isolation from the others. But as you see, Leonardo abandoned this tradition and he may have been encouraged to do so by the accounts in the Synoptic Gospels: In St Matthew we read, after the announcement of the betrayal, that Christ said 'he, that dippeth his hand with me in the dish, the same shall betray me.' In St Mark we read that Jesus said 'one of you which eateth with me shall betray me ... it is one of the twelve, that dippeth with me in the dish.' And in St Luke 'behold, the hand of him that betrayeth me is with me on the table.' It seems likely that Leonardo took his cue from this version, conspicuously showing the hand of Judas on the table quite close to that of Christ, while most of the other apostles don't have their hands on the table at all.[21]

The rapid sketch also testifies to the fact that Leonardo really painted Saint John and not Mary Magdalene. In this sketch each of the disciples are labeled, including Saint John.

---

[19] Jn. 13:23.

[20] Edersheim, *The Temple: Its Ministry and Services as They Were at the Time of Jesus Christ*, 156.

[21] Gombrich, "Papers Given on the Occasion of the Dedication of the Last Supper (after Leonardo)." It is imperative to point out that the sop dipped which the Lord gave to Judas (Jn. 13:26) is not the Eucharist. Rather it was the "Haroseth" (a compound of dates, raisins, and vinegar to symbolize the mortar of Egypt) which was eaten at the beginning of the Paschal Meal. After the Haroseth, Judas "went out immediately" (Jn. 13:30). (cf. Edersheim, *The Temple: Its Ministry and Services as They Were at the Time of Jesus Christ*, 157, 162).

Furthermore, Brown's assertions that Jesus and "his bride" are joined at the hip and are sitting in such a way as to display the letter "V" (allegedly a sign of the chalice) and the letter "M" (for Mary Magdalene, or marriage, or something else), are also false, since one "can take any great painting and play this kind of game with it."[22] Saint John is leaning away from the Lord because he is speaking with Saint Peter who, at this point as depicted by Leonardo, is motioning to Saint John. We have established that the figure on Jesus' right is not Mary Magdalene, so Saint Peter is not slicing his hand across her neck as Brown falsely states; but with his hand, he is motioning to Saint John to ask the Lord who it is that will betray Him. Again Professor Gombrich's analysis of this scene is most accurate:

> The figures on both sides of Our Lord may be considered by threes together and thus each of them appears as a unity relating both within the group and with its neighbour. Next to Christ, on the right hand, are John, Judas and Peter. Peter, who is the farthest away, having heard the words of the Lord, rises quickly, in keeping with his vehement character, behind Judas who, terrified and looking upwards, leans over the table tightly gripping the purse in his right hand but making, with his left, an involuntary convulsive movement as if to say 'What does this mean? What is to happen?' Peter in the meantime has grasped with his left hand the right shoulder of John who is leaning towards him, and—at the same time pointing to Christ—signals to the favourite disciple that he should ask who is the traitor.[23]

With reference to Brown's claims of a disembodied hand holding a dagger next to the group of disciples around Saint Peter, the truth is that this hand is not disembodied. "Both a preliminary drawing by Leonardo and early copies of "The Last Supper" show that the hand and dagger belong to Peter—a reference to a passage in the Gospel of St. John, in which Peter draws a sword in defense of Jesus."[24]

---

[22] *Seattle Pacific University Magazine*, "Decoding The Da Vinci Code: The Challenge of Historic Christianity to Post-Modern Fantasy."

[23] Gombrich, "Papers Given on the Occasion of the Dedication of the Last Supper (after Leonardo)."

[24] Boucher, "Does The Da Vinci Code Crack Leonardo?"

Now there is one more error in Dan Brown's interpretation: *The Last Supper* is not a fresco, but it is tempera painted on stone or a dry wall. This accounts for its massive deterioration in just a few years after it was painted. After many attempts to restore and save *The Last Supper*, it is almost certain that nothing of what Leonardo originally painted on that wall is still there.[25] In other words, Brown's notion that Mary Magdalene is seated on Jesus' right is not based what Leonardo originally painted, but on the personal interpretations of those who attempted to restore the work. Finally, Victoria Alexander highlights the absurdity of Brown's peculiar claims saying:

> My nagging question: If da Vinci's The Last Supper was a commissioned work—that took 4 years to complete—what was the reaction when it was finally displayed? Did townspeople ask: Okay, that's Jesus' red-haired wife, what apostle skipped the last supper? Were people enraged at the symbolism or were they too stupid to figure out that The Beloved Apostle John was really Mary Magdalene?[26]

3. Dan's Deceptions about Mary Magdalene as the Head of the Church

- In the [Gnostic] gospels, Jesus suspects that He will soon be captured and crucified. So He gives Mary Magdalene instructions on how to carry on His Church after He is gone. As a result, Peter expresses discontent over playing second fiddle to a woman. I daresay Peter was something of a sexist (*DVC*, 268).
- It was not Peter to whom Christ gave directions with which to establish the Christian Church. It was Mary Magdalene (*DVC*, 268).
- Jesus was the original feminist. He intended for the future of His Church to be in the hands of Mary Magdalene (*DVC*, 268).
- The threat Mary Magdalene posed to men of the early Church was potentially ruinous. Not only was she the woman to whom Jesus had assigned the task of founding the Church, but she also had physi-

[25] *The Da Vinci Code Deception* DVD.
[26] Alexander, "The Da Vinci Code."

cal proof that the Church's newly proclaimed *deity* had spawned a mortal bloodline (*DVC*, 274).

- ... the quest for the Holy Grail has always been a quest for Magdalene — the wronged Queen, entombed with proof of her family's rightful claim to power (*DVC*, 278).

The Truth that Mary Magdalene was Never Chosen as the Head of the Church

What really does not make sense in all of this is Brown's insistence that Mary Magdalene is the divine mother (*DVC*, 275): If, as Brown believes, Mary Magdalene is a goddess and Jesus is mortal, why then would she have been in need to receive His authority in order to head the Church? As goddess, would she not have had authority over Him? How could a goddess receive instructions on how to run the Church from a mere mortal? Brown's theories simply do not add up.

Dan Brown's concept of Mary Magdalene as the head of the Church is completely unfounded, and once again there is no biblical or historical evidence to verify his claims. The Lord Jesus Christ explicitly chose twelve disciples, and later seventy, but Mary Magdalene is not mentioned anywhere in the Holy Bible as being one of these. We acknowledge Mary Magdalene as an exemplary follower of the Lord Jesus Christ. She is commended for following the Lord at every step of his Passion, Crucifixion, and Death; demonstrating her courage and great love for Him as her Savior, and acknowledging Him as her God and the Lord of all. She is also given a position of prominence as the first to speak to the risen Lord after His Resurrection. The Holy Orthodox Church does, however, reject the suggestion that she was given the authority of presbyter, or that she held any episcopal office.

The New Testament provides evidence that the Church was founded by Christ Himself and that the Church's leadership on Earth was given *only* to the twelve disciples (and later seventy more apostles):

- And when He had called His twelve disciples to *Him*, He gave them power *over* unclean spirits, to cast them out, and to heal all kinds of sickness and all kinds of disease. Now the names of the twelve apostles are these: first, Simon, who is called Peter, and Andrew his brother; James the *son* of Zebedee, and John his brother; Philip and Bartholomew; Thomas and Matthew the tax collector; James the son of Alphaeus, and Lebbaeus, whose surname was Thaddaeus; Simon the Canaanite, and Judas Iscariot, who also betrayed Him. These twelve Jesus sent out... (Matt. 10:1–5; cf. also Mk. 6:7; Lk. 6:13–16; and Lk. 9:1–2 which give a very similar account).

- So Jesus said to them, "Assuredly I say to you, that in the regeneration, when the Son of Man sits on the throne of His glory, you who have followed Me will also sit on twelve thrones, judging the twelve tribes of Israel" (Matt. 19:28).
- "But you are those who have continued with Me in My trials. And I bestow upon you a kingdom, just as My Father bestowed *one* upon Me, that you may eat and drink at My table in My kingdom, and sit on thrones judging the twelve tribes of Israel" (Lk. 22:28–30).
- When He had said this, He showed them *His* hands and His side. Then the disciples were glad when they saw the Lord. So Jesus said to them again, "Peace to you! As the Father has sent Me, I also send you." And when He had said this, He breathed on *them*, and said to them, "Receive the Holy Spirit. "If you forgive the sins of any, they are forgiven them; if you retain the *sins* of any, they are retained" (Jn. 20:20–23).
- The Lord appointed seventy others also, and sent them two by two before His face into every city and place where He Himself was about to go... Then the seventy returned with joy, saying, "Lord, even the demons are subject to us in Your name" (Lk. 10:1, 17).

As we can clearly see in the above, Mary Magdalene was not given the authority of priesthood, leadership, papacy, or any official position in the Church. At the Last Supper also, Jesus celebrated only with "the twelve;"[27] so if Jesus intended for the future of His Church to be in the

[27] Matt. 26:20; Mk. 14:17; Lk. 22:14; and Jn. 13.

hands of Mary Magdalene, should we not expect that He would have invited her to the Institution of the Eucharist? Her exclusion from the Lord's Supper clearly indicates that she was never selected for this role.

Moreover, for Brown to boldly claim that Mary Magdalene was the original head of the Church effectively denies the apostolic succession of the Church. Apostolic succession is the continuing line of descent from the disciples of Jesus Christ to the present-day Church, transmitted through episcopal consecration. In simpler terms, the disciples appointed bishops as their successors, and their successors in turn had consecrated other bishops. In this way the apostolate was kept alive in the episcopacy, and this became a guarantee of truth and grace.[28] Saint Irenaeus discusses apostolic succession in his *Against Heresies* saying:

> In this order, and by this succession, the ecclesiastical tradition from the apostles, and the preaching of the truth, have come down to us. And this is most abundant proof that there is one and the same life-giving faith, which has been preserved in the Church from the apostles until now, and handed down in truth... Wherefore it is incumbent to obey the presbyters who are in the Church—those who, as I have shown, possess the succession from the apostles; those who, together with the succession of the episcopate, have received the certain gift of truth, according to the good pleasure of the Father...

Saint Irenaeus then continues with the following, which can be said of Dan Brown:

> But it is also incumbent to hold in suspicion others who depart from the primitive succession... looking upon them as heretics of perverse minds, or as schismatics puffed up and self-pleasing, or again as hypocrites, acting thus for the sake of money and vainglory. For all these have fallen from the truth.[29]

As the witnesses of the Lord's ministry, death, and Resurrection, and as the representatives of the ascended Christ, the disciples themselves are credited with accurately preaching what Jesus taught. "Their voice has

---

[28] Douglas, *The New International Dictionary of the Christian Church*, 59–60.

[29] Saint Irenaeus, *Against Heresies*, *ANF*, 1.497.

gone out through all the earth, And their words to the end of the world," and certainly, they are the ones who restored the world to the knowledge of the truth. The disciples of the apostles are the Apostolic Fathers who took the Christian faith directly from them, upheld the Gospel of Christ, and who ensured the constancy of the upright and Orthodox doctrines. To say that Jesus Christ charged Mary Magdalene with these responsibilities eliminates the authenticity of apostolic succession and inaccurately deems it false.

It also necessary to clarify that Jesus Christ did not intend for Saint Peter to be the sole leader of the Church. Saints Peter and Paul established the Church in Rome, Saint Peter also established the Church of Antioch, and Saint Mark founded the Church of Alexandria. Here Brown has yet again viewed the entire Christian Church as the Roman Catholic Church, and has again fallen into subsequent error.

4. Dan's Deceptions about Mary Magdalene, the Sacred Feminine, and the Goddess

Sophie refers to Mary Magdalene as "The prostitute" to which Teabing replies:

- Magdalene was no such thing. That unfortunate misconception is the legacy of a smear campaign launched by the early Church. The Church needed to defame Mary Magdalene in order to cover up her dangerous secret—her role as the Holy Grail (*DVC*, 263–4).
- Mary Magdalene was of royal descent... Magdalene was recast as a whore in order to erase evidence of her powerful family ties (*DVC*, 269).
- Mary Magdalene... [is] the Goddess, the Holy Grail, and the Divine Mother (*DVC*, 275).
- The quest for the Holy Grail is literally the quest to kneel before the bones of Mary Magdalene. A journey to pray at the feet of the outcast one, the lost sacred feminine (*DVC*, 277).
- The days of the goddess were over... Mother Earth had become a man's world, and the gods of destruction and war were taking their

toll. The male ego had spent two millennia running unchecked by its female counterpart... it was this obliteration of the sacred feminine in modern life that had caused... "life out of balance" — an unstable situation marked by... a growing disrespect for Mother Earth (*DVC*, 135).

- Early religion was based on the divine order of Nature. The goddess Venus and the planet Venus were one and the same. The goddess had a place in the nighttime sky and was known by many names — Venus, the Eastern Star, Ishtar, Astarte — all of them powerful female concepts with ties to Nature and Mother Earth (*DVC*, 40).
- Women once celebrated as an essential half of spiritual enlightenment, had been banished from the temples of the world. There were no female Orthodox rabbis, Catholic priests, nor Islamic clerics (*DVC*, 134).

The Truth about Mary Magdalene, the Sacred Feminine, and the Goddess

For Dan Brown, Mary Magdalene is the embodiment of the lost sacred feminine, who was oppressed and eliminated by the Roman Catholic Church. Brown claims that very early in the Church, Mary Magdalene was viewed as the divine mother, and as the mother of the child of Jesus Christ; therefore her role as the Holy Grail posed a serious threat to the authority of the Church. And so, Brown contends, the Church recast Mary Magdalene as a prostitute in order to eliminate her position and power. Again, this is all a farrago of nonsense. There are three prominent women named Mary in the New Testament: 1) Saint Mary, the Mother of Jesus Christ; 2) Mary of Bethany, the sister of Lazarus and Martha; and 3) Mary Magdalene. In the Gospel of Saint John, Mary of Bethany is described as anointing Jesus' feet and wiping them with her hair.[30] In the Gospel of Luke, another woman also anoints Jesus' feet,

[30] Jn. 11:2; 12:3.

but she is known as the sinful woman.[31] Then in the very next chapter of his gospel, Saint Luke mentions that Mary Magdalene is the woman from whom the Lord Jesus Christ cast out seven demons.[32] So Brown's idea of Mary Magdalene as a prostitute is not based on biblical fact; and actually it came to be in 591, when Roman Catholic Pope Gregory announced that Mary Magdalene, Mary of Bethany, and the sinful woman were one and the same person. The Holy Orthodox Church has never held this view; but in 1969 the Roman Catholic Church corrected the error, stating that these women were three individuals.

In *The Da Vinci Code*, Brown repeatedly attempts to change our understanding of Mary Magdalene radically. His main goal is to make the reader believe that she is the goddess. Brown considers Mary Magdalene to be the archetypal feminine; she is the lost goddess who should be worshipped together with Venus or any other goddesses, as the equal female counterpart of God. As well as arguing for her reinstatement into the primacy in the Church, Brown also contends that Mary Magdalene's rightful position as "the goddess" must be restored in order to bring back a healthy balance to the Earth which has been destroyed by the single, all-male Deity. On page 479 Brown writes that "We are starting to sense the dangers of our history... and of our destructive paths. We are beginning to sense the need to restore the sacred feminine." Yet again, Brown lifts these ideas from his primary sources. In this case, it is Margaret Starbird in her book *The Woman with the Alabaster Jar*, who gives Brown his ideas about of "life out of balance," and states that the only way to restore the world is to recognize Mary Magdalene as the lost goddess. Starbird writes: "The Grail, we suggest, is the lost feminine — the Sister-Bride of Christianity, the wife of Jesus. What would our world be like if the Bride in Christianity had never been lost? And what will it be like when she is restored?"[33]

My strong assertion is that nothing in our world will improve as a result of Mary Magdalene being "restored" as goddess, because in real-

[31] Lk. 7:37–8.

[32] Lk. 8:2.

[33] Starbird, *The Woman with the Alabaster Jar*, 157.

ity, she is not a goddess. Mary Magdalene is not divine. She was quite simply an ordinary female who lived, died, and was buried; and whose body was subject to corruption as all other human beings. During her life on Earth, Mary Magdalene did nothing to manifest her alleged divinity, and she did not perform any miracles to prove her deity. Even the Holy Bible and the Fathers of the Church make no reference to Mary Magdalene as the sacred feminine. This argument aside, the fundamental question remains: If Mary Magdalene is goddess how then could she have died? If she is a goddess, after all, one would expect her to be eternal. What astounds me the most, is not so much Brown's preposterous beliefs, but the willingness of a gullible mass-market to follow his theories which are based on poor evidence and poor logic. The majority of those who have read *The Da Vinci Code*, particularly western women, have blindly accepted Brown's flawed conclusions without questioning their validity. The reason for this is Brown's repetition of accusations against the so-called misogynistic hierarchy that oppressed women; in a contemporary age dominated by feminist rhetoric and a push for feminist rights, Brown's ideas seem believable even if they make no sense. If people would only stop and assess Brown's claims, they would realize that Mary Magdalene, Venus, or any other goddess has absolutely nothing to offer. The goddess cannot hear or answer prayers. The goddess cannot give true inner peace and serenity. The goddess cannot liberate the mind, body, and spirit from the bondage of sin. The goddess cannot grant the type of everlasting joy which can never be taken away. The goddess cannot forgive sins. And most importantly, the goddess cannot grant eternal life or eternal rest "in the place out of which grief, sorrow, and groaning have fled away in the light of [Christ's] saints."[34] One of the other disturbing fallacies in Dan Brown's work is his claim that the rightful return of the goddess will elevate the status of women, resulting in a more egalitarian society. But as Amy Welborn points out, this is not the case:

---

[34] From the Diptych of The Divine Liturgy of Saint Basil the Great in the Coptic Orthodox Church (cf. *The Three Coptic Divine Liturgies*, 346).

> I have to question his [Brown'] conclusions, that somehow a society that worships both male and female deities somehow has consequences that are egalitarian; that are more just for women. This is simply not true. When you look at cultures that do worship both male and female deities, you don't find any kind of increase in the equality of women or the position of women, in fact you might find the exact opposite, because in most situations the entrance of Christianity into a culture has done nothing but elevate the position of women in that culture.[35]

Dan Brown repeatedly and strongly espouses the practice of worshipping the goddess. On the last page of *The Da Vinci Code*, Robert Langdon worships the bones of Mary Magdalene at her alleged burial place under the *Inverted Pyramid* at the Louvre Museum in Paris:[36] "With a sudden upwelling of reverence [he] fell to his knees. For a moment, he thought he heard a woman's voice ... the wisdom of the ages ... whispering up from the chasms of the earth" (*DVC*, 489). But for what reason is Mary Magdalene, the goddess, worthy of glorification? The goddess is not the Creator of the universe, or the Sustainer of the universe, or the Redeemer of all humanity, or the Savior of the world, or the Lover of Mankind; the goddess did not trample upon death and abolish it, so for what reason should she be praised? Only the one True God is the author of all of these things, therefore He is the only One to Whom we worthily ascribe all due glorification, worship, and reverence. Dan Brown refers to Mary Magdalene as "the wisdom of the ages" but again I ask: Who is the Wisdom of the ages and "the Ancient of Days"[37] except God Himself alone? As Saint Paul explains: "Christ is the power of God and the Wisdom of God;"[38] and as Saint Justin Martyr also declares: "The Word of Wisdom ... is Himself this God begotten of the Father of all things ... [He is] Word, and Wisdom, and Power, and the Glory of the Begetter."[39]

---

[35] *The Da Vinci Code Deception* DVD.

[36] Mary Magdalene is not buried under the Inverted Pyramid; this is just another of Brown's inventions, and actually the location of her remains is not certain.

[37] Dan. 7:9.

[38] 1 Cor. 1:24.

[39] Saint Justin Martyr, *Dialogue with Trypho*, *ANF*, 1.227.

As we have stated, Brown insists that the practice of worshipping a goddess, or multiple goddesses, has been eliminated from the Church and "modern religion," but interestingly he accuses Islam and Judaism of the same. Through his attack on Islam for not having female clerics, and Judaism for not having female rabbis, Brown too blames these religions for the banishment of the goddess and the demise of the sacred feminine. However, in both *Angels and Demons* and *The Da Vinci Code*, he sets out to reverse all of this.

We find much evidence of the sacred feminine in ancient worlds and in early cultures, especially among those outside the influence of monotheistic faiths. Fertility and nature goddesses abounded in the ancient world and spread across a variety of cultures; and they were often very much the same in everything except name.[40] For example, the Aramaeans of Syria revered Hadad as the chief god of Damascus, and beside him was his consort Athtar.[41] Isis the Ancient Egyptian queen of the heavens was the counterpart of her husband Osiris, god of the underworld. Anahita, a major goddess of the Persians, was regarded as the consort of Mithra and was worshipped as far as India and Rome. Astarte was the Phoenician goddess of fertility and reproduction; and she was adopted by the Ancient Greeks as Aphrodite, the goddess of love. The Romans borrowed most of their gods and goddesses from the ancient Greeks but gave them different names, so Aphrodite became Venus, the goddess of the hunt, fertility and childbirth; she was the female twin of the Greco-Roman god Apollo. In Norse mythology, Freyja was worshipped as a fertility goddess and the counterpart to her brother the fertility god Freyr, and the list goes on.[42] Other cultures to this day also openly regard the feminine principle as an essential element: The Earth goddess Asase Yaa, of the Ashanti in Ghana, is the companion of Nyame the sky god; and she is offered first fruits at harvest time. In eastern Nigerian mythology, Ala the daughter of the great god Chuku, is the Earth mother, the guardian of the harvest, and the goddess of

---

[40] *Channel4*, "The Sacred Feminine: Father Sun, Mother Earth."

[41] *A Lion Handbook: The World's Religions*, 67.

[42] *Channel4*, "The Sacred Feminine: Father Sun, Mother Earth."

fertility for humans and animals.[43] In Hinduism — one of the few larger religions not to have wholly excluded the sacred feminine — each of the principal gods has both a male and female side, and the female aspect of the gods is known as the "shakti."[44] Hinduism's three major gods all have female counterparts: there is Sarasvati, the goddess of knowledge, who is the consort of Brahma; Lakshmi, the goddess of wealth and good fortune, who is the wife of Vishnu; and Kali, the "great mother" who is consort of the male god Shiva.[45]

All of these goddesses represent the age-old worship of Mother Nature and this is precisely what Brown hopes to reintroduce. He is calling the world to return to pre-Christian, neo-pagan pantheism where "no human incarnations are worshipped in particular, as all of nature and the universe are considered embodiments of God and Goddess, or of gods and goddesses, worthy of respect, reverence, or worship."[46] Neo-pagan pantheism is the belief in gods and goddesses as a duality. It is a faith where many believe there are countless spirit beings, and gods and goddesses within all of nature — God is all and within all; all are one god. It is a belief system where the Great Mother Earth, or Mother Nature, is highly worshipped.[47] Dr. Michael Green rightly observes that:

> The sacred feminine really means the reign of Mother Nature ... The sacred feminine assures us that everything in Nature, including our inner self, is divine ... And despite all the comforting imagery of the Mother Goddess from whom everything emerges and to whom everything returns, she is no God ... The "sacred feminine" is a giant con for the gullible.[48]

By calling for the return of the goddess, Brown is simply advocating a

---

[43] Ibid.

[44] Wilkinson, *Illustrated Dictionary of Religions: Figures, Festivals, and Beliefs of the World's Religions*, 36.

[45] Ibid.; *A Lion Handbook: The World's Religions*, 184.

[46] "What Neo-Pagans Believe." Accessed at www.beliefnet.com/story/80/story_8058_1.html.

[47] Ibid.

[48] Green, *The Books the Church Suppressed: Fiction and Truth in The Da Vinci Code*, 170, 174.

new do-it-yourself spirituality. He is pushing for a religion where one can believe in any range of beliefs, gods or goddesses, but with one exception: one can choose any type of spirituality which s/he likes, as long as it is not orthodox Christianity. In other words, Brown wants a single world religion which unites all beliefs under Nature and the Goddess.[49] As we have seen, Brown has used lies and empty theories to prove that the sacred feminine and Mary Magdalene as the divine mother is to be worshipped instead of Jesus Christ. But we, on the other hand, have no reason to bemoan the demise of the goddess, and we have no cause to resurrect her in modern society or in the Church. In trying to reintroduce goddess worship into the world, Brown is severely mistaken: the goddess is not to be worshipped, but in truth, "at the name of Jesus every knee should bow, of those in heaven, and of those on earth, and of those under the earth, and ... every tongue should confess that Jesus Christ is Lord, to the glory of God the Father."[50]

5. Dan's Deceptions about the Hieros Gamos and Sexual Union

On page 569 of *Angels and Demons*, Brown suggests that sexual intercourse is "a religious experience."

- Hieros Gamos ... dates back more than two thousand years. Egyptian priests and priestesses performed it regularly to celebrate the reproductive power of the female ... It means *sacred marriage* ... [Although it] probably looked like a sex ritual, Hieros Gamos had nothing to do with eroticism. It was a spiritual act (*DVC*, 334–5).
- Historically, intercourse was the act through which male and female experienced God. The ancients believed that the male was spiritually incomplete until he had carnal knowledge of the sacred feminine. Physical union with the female remained the sole means through which man could become spiritually complete and ulti-

[49] Ibid., 171.
[50] Phil. 2:10–11.

mately achieve *gnosis*—knowledge of the divine. Since the days of Isis, sex rites had been considered man's only bridge from earth to heaven (*DVC*, 335).

- Admittedly, the concept of sex as a pathway to God was mind-boggling at first... early Jewish tradition involved ritualistic sex. *In the Temple, no less*... Men seeking spiritual wholeness came to the temple to visit priestesses—or hierodules—with whom they made love and experienced the divine through physical union (*DVC*, 336).
- By communing with woman... man could achieve a climactic instant when his mind when totally blank and he could see God... A moment of clarity during which God could be glimpsed (*DVC*, 335).
- Intercourse was the revered union of the two halves of the human spirit—male and female—through which the male could find spiritual wholeness and communion with God (*DVC*, 335).
- [Hieros Gamos] was not about sex, it was about spirituality. The Hieros Gamos is not a perversion. It's a deeply sacrosanct ceremony (*DVC*, 335).
- The Church... worked hard to demonize sex and recast it as a disgusting and sinful act... Our ancient heritage and our very physiologies tell us sex is natural—a cherished route to spiritual fulfillment—and yet modern religion decries it as shameful, teaching us to fear our sexual desire as the hand of the devil (*DVC*, 336).

The Truth about the Hieros Gamos and Sexual Union

Before *The Da Vinci Code*, Dan Brown introduced the notion of sexual union between a man and woman outside the context of Christian marriage as a religious experience in his first Robert Langdon thriller, *Angels and Demons*. This thought was a subtle allusion to the idea of gnosis of the divine through intercourse, which is at the core of *The Da Vinci Code*. Although *The Da Vinci Code* is not a sex book per se, there are plenty of ideas about sexuality in the book, and in fact, it centers on sexuality. As is evident in the excerpts above, Brown asserts that the act of sexual intercourse is where man can find divinity and the knowledge of God. To ensure that the reader has understood the true essence of his position on sexual intercourse, Brown introduces the "hieros gamos," or the "sacred marriage." His description of the hieros gamos is the most graphic scene in *The Da Vinci Code*, where we read of how masked men and women dressed in black and white engage in sexual intercourse on an altar, in honour of women and the goddess. Brown claims that the hieros gamos was the central rite of pre-Christian pagan goddess worship, and that it was the Church that recast it as a shameful act. But, as we have noted, "the goddesses did not dominate the pre-Christian world—not in the religions of Rome, her barbarian subjects, Egypt, or even Semitic lands where the hieros gamos was an ancient practice. Nor did the Hellenized cult of Isis appear to have included sex in its secret rites."[51] The book's main female character, Sophie Neveu inadvertently walks in on a hieros gamos ceremony which was being performed in the basement of a country château by her grandfather, Jacques Saunière. She is so shocked by what she sees that she cuts off all communication with him for ten years. We then read of how Robert Langdon re-educates Sophie's way of thinking about evil, and convinces her that the hieros gamos is not an evil satanic sex ritual, but a deeply spiritual and holy ceremony. The hieros gamos is mentioned in *The Templar Revelation*, *The Woman with the Alabaster Jar*, and *The Goddess in the Gospels*. Although Brown does not claim that Jesus Christ and Mary Magdalene were involved in a "sacred marriage" (as his sources state), he does rely heavily on these books for his ideas about the ritual.

There are three primary responses to Brown's claims about the hieros gamos and sexual intercourse: 1) Sexual intercourse is not used to worship women. In Brown's description of the hieros gamos (on page 338), the participants in the ritual honour the goddess with the following words:

> I was with you in the beginning, in the dawn of all that is holy, I bore you from the womb before the start of day…

[51] Miesel, "Dismantling *The Da Vinci Code*."

> The woman whom you behold is love! …
> She has her dwelling in eternity!

The Templar Revelation quotes Hildegrad of Bingen (1098–1178) using these very same words when describing a vision of the goddess saying:

> Then I seemed to see a girl of surpassing radiant beauty, with such dazzling brightness streaming from her face that I could not behold her fully. She wore a cloak whiter than snow, brighter than stars, her shoes were of pure gold … On her breast she had an ivory tablet, on which appeared in shades of sapphire the image of a man. And all creation called this girl sovereign lady. The girl began to speak to the image on her breast: I was with you in the beginning, in the dawn of all that is holy, I bore you from the womb before the start of day." And I heard a voice saying to me "The girl whom you behold is Love: she has her dwelling in eternity."[52]

Here Brown steals the attributes of God, applies them to the goddess, and uses them to worship her. For, Who is "in the beginning" (Gen. 1:1; Jn. 1:1–2) except the Almighty God alone? Who has "His dwelling in eternity" (Isa. 57:15) but the Lord of Hosts? And Who alone "is Love" (1 Jn 4:8) save for God Himself? The Holy Orthodox Church, as we have said, rejects the worship of the goddess; no less the worship of the goddess through sexual intercourse with epithets reserved only for God.

2) Sexual intercourse is not a sacrament and never has been a means of achieving "gnosis." Dan Brown claims that in the climactic instant during sexual intercourse man's mind goes completely blank, and so he glimpses God. But I ask Brown: In what form does man see God in this split second? What type of gnosis is achieved at this instant? What *exactly* does man learn about God at this point? As you can see, Brown's theory hinges upon stupidity; he avoids these issues because they destroy his theory. The Holy Orthodox Church has never taught that revelation or knowledge of God is achieved in altered states of consciousness during sexual intercourse. Rather, we believe that God reveals Himself to us primarily though the Scriptures and through the seven holy sacraments of the Church. Prayer, the assistance and guid-

---

[52] Picknett and Prince, *The Templar Revelation*, 212–3.

ance of our father of confession, the teachings of presbyters and bishops of the Church, are other means through which we also acquire knowledge of God. The Church teaches that one can find "spiritual wholeness and communion with God" through Repentance and Confession, Holy Communion, observance of God's statutes, and a healthy spiritual life in Christ, and not, as Brown purports, through sexual intercourse. Brown uses the ideas of sex for gnosis, and sex as the route to spirituality as an excuse for full sexual permissiveness. What he is really doing is presenting sexual union for sexual ecstasy under the guise of physical union for spiritual ecstasy. In other words, full sexual freedom should be permitted because its real purpose is to achieve gnosis. It is all part of his shallow "return to paganism" agenda.

3) The Church has not recast sex as a shameful act; the Church believes that sex it not shameful as long as it is within the context of Christian marriage. The Holy Bible repeatedly emphasizes that sexual union within Christian marriage is good if used as a safeguard against fornication or adultery and for procreation; though it only remains good within the confines of that marriage. In other words, the purpose of sexual intercourse in marriage is twofold: Firstly, to prevent sexual intercourse outside of marriage; and secondly, as a result of sexual intercourse in marriage, to produce children from time to time. The Early Church Fathers and writers have much to say on the topic of sexual intercourse and marriage. Lactantius states: "Sexual desire [is given] for the procreation of offspring.[53] And in the *Constitutions of the Holy Apostles* we read the following: "We believe that lawful marriage, and the begetting of children, is honourable and undefiled; for difference of sexes was formed in Adam and Eve for the increase of mankind."[54] Therefore, the teaching of the Holy Orthodox Church holds sexual union in marriage as honorable, though it does not ascribe honor to the fertility rite for sexual pleasure which *The Da Vinci Code* portrays. Saint Paul in his First Epistle to the Corinthians says:

---

[53] Lactantius, *The Divine Institutes*, *ANF*, 7:185.

[54] *Constitutions of the Holy Apostles*, *ANF*, 7:454.

> Do not deprive one another except with consent for a time, that you may give yourselves to fasting and prayer; and come together again so that Satan does not tempt you because of your lack of self-control. But I say this as a concession, not as a commandment. For I wish that all men were even as I myself. But each one has his own gift from God, one in this manner and another in that. But I say to the unmarried and to the widows: It is good for them if they remain even as I am; but if they cannot exercise self-control, let them marry. For it is better to marry than to burn *with passion*.[55]

This means the Holy Orthodox Church teaches that in marriage, sexual desire can be fulfilled in order to protect people from sexual immorality: For the unmarried who need to fulfill their sexual desires, sexual intercourse in marriage is given to prevent fornication. And for the married who cannot exercise self-control, sexual intercourse is given in the marriage relationship to prevent adultery. Sexual intercourse outside of marriage, any type of unnatural sexual acts within or without of marriage, or any sex rituals, are referred to by the Holy Bible as adultery or fornication; and it warns against both in the Old and New Testaments. Saint Paul in Hebrews writes: "Marriage *is* honorable among all, and the bed undefiled; but fornicators and adulterers God will judge."[56] The Bible teaches that when sexuality is misused, it becomes a source of sin and immorality. Based on the teachings of the Bible then, it is fair to conclude that the sex ritual depicted in *The Da Vinci Code* is a type of fornication; and so it is condemned by the Holy Orthodox Church. Although we teach that sex within marriage is holy, it is only holy if it is a private act between one man and one woman; that is, a husband and his wife. In the sacrament of marriage the husband and the wife become one flesh; the Church respects this union and considers it blessed, so sexual activity within this union should only be reserved for those whom God has joined. For this reason the Church forbids all group sex acts such as the hieros gamos. As Saint Matthew the Evangelist explains: "But I say to you that whoever looks at a woman to lust for her

[55] 1 Cor. 7:5–9.
[56] Heb. 13:4.

has already committed adultery with her in his heart."[57] Therefore, the Church also forbids the observation of rituals like the hieros gamos or the act of people involved in sexual intercourse, for in so doing the observers themselves become participants in the act. It is for this reason that the Church also does not permit the watching or pornographic or erotic television programs.

In *The Da Vinci Code*, we learn that the character, Jacques Saunière, participated in the hieros gamos while his wife was still living. Thus, not only does Brown promote participation in sex rituals—which are sources of sin for the unmarried—but he also alludes to the fact that participation in such rituals is acceptable for those who are married. For Dan Brown, adultery, fornication, and complete sexual freedom are not evil. Euteneuer gives a succinct assessment of the hieros gamos saying: "What Dan Brown calls hieros gamos, an ancient pagan "sacred marriage" ceremony, is nothing other than a perverse mockery of holy matrimony depicted in living color in the pages of Brown's book. If this act was "sacred" it was only so to the devil."[58]

Very briefly, on the point of Brown's claim that ritualistic sex was sanctioned in Solomon's Temple, this is another fallacy stolen directly from Picknett and Prince.[59] The Hebrews were extremely careful not to defile the house of God, acting in accordance with the laws given to them by God Himself. In the Book of Deuteronomy, Moses warns the Jews saying: "You shall not bring the wages of a harlot or the price of a dog to the house of the LORD your God for any vowed offering, for both of these *are* an abomination to the LORD your God."[60] So as is evident, Brown's claim that early Jews practiced ritual sex with priestesses is unsubstantiated. The hierodules to which Brown refers, were actually pagan slaves dedicated to the service of a god. These hierodules lived in the pagan temples in the areas surrounding the Israelites, and practiced ritual prostitution there. However, they did not practice sex in

---

[57] Matt. 5:28.

[58] Euteneuer, "The Da Vinci Mess—Part I: Sanitizing Satanism."

[59] Picknett and Prince, The Templar Revelation, 339.

[60] Deut. 23:18.

Solomon's Temple, and there are no historical records showing any era in which such acts occurred.

CHAPTER NINE

Conclusions

> A time is coming when men will go mad, and when they see someone who is not mad, they will attack him saying, "You are mad, you are not like us."
>
> Saint Abba Anthony, the Great[1]

In time, the hype and propaganda surrounding Dan Brown's number one bestselling novels,[2] *Angels and Demons* and *The Da Vinci Code*, will fade away into the dust. And indeed, the memory of these novels themselves will soon disappear into oblivion. Or will they? Will all of the challenging religious, spiritual, Theological, Christological, and historical questions raised in *Angels and Demons* and *The Da Vinci Code* come to be forgotten? Or will they continue to lure those who are unsuspecting and unknowledgeable into Dan Brown's trap? Of this we cannot be certain. But the seeds of inquiry have been planted; the motion has started. Unfortunately, in today's world where there is a thirst for spirituality, Dan Brown is directing the naïve in the wrong direction. He is leading them through the wide gate and onto the broad way that leads to destruction.[3] Instead of telling them that God, the Father of the Lord, God and Savior Jesus Christ, is the only One who can satisfy their longing and fill their emptiness, he tells them that the truth is within themselves. Rather than teach humanity of the overwhelming spiritual joy which comes from worshipping and praising the Lord of Hosts, he tells them to worship the sacred feminine that only troubles and makes anxious the human spirit. Instead of telling people of the sublime life

---

[1] Ward, *The Sayings of the Desert Fathers: The Alphabetical Collection*, 6.

[2] "In early 2004, all four of Dan Brown's novels held spots on the *New York Times* bestseller list during the same week." (cf. www.danbrown.com/ meet_dan/index.html).

[3] Matt. 7:13

of purity and holiness, he encourages complete sexual permissiveness through sexual immorality which utterly destroys the soul. Rather than show people how the Church can lead them to God, he tells people to look for God in sexual intercourse. I could easily go on about the false alternatives to the truth which Dan Brown, like a serpent, has injected into the minds of a new generation of seekers.

By claiming to initiate people into a secret knowledge, and by presenting himself as the all-knowing informant of global conspiracies, Brown has gained the trust of millions through the use of lies. What is most frightening though, is that people are willing to cast aside four millennia of human history, more than two-thousand years of Christian truth, the wisdom of previous generations, and the upright teachings of Fathers of the Church, for a sensationalized set of lies and empty beliefs. Many people have overlooked what is perhaps one of the most dangerous ideas in *The Da Vinci Code*; and it speaks to this very point. It comes when Teabing declares:

> In terms of prophecy ... we are currently in an epoch of enormous change. The millennium has recently passed, and with it has ended the two-thousand-year-long astrological Age of Pisces — the fish, which is also the sign of Jesus. As any astrological symbologist will tell you, the Piscean ideal believes that man must be *told* what to do by higher power because man is incapable of thinking for himself. Hence it has been a time of fervent religion. Now, however, we are entering the Age of Aquarius—the water bearer—whose ideals claim that man will learn the *truth* and be able to think for himself. This ideological shift is enormous, and it is occurring right now (*DVC*, 289–90).[4]

The Age of Aquarius is said to be a "new age" which will bring about a kind of anarchic world where there is no hierarchical structure. In other words, we do not need the Church, we do not need God; we possess the answers to the knowledge of the truth because we are all gods! These ideas of false freedom can be extremely enticing, and so

[4] As one who is a lover of the sacred feminine, it is surprising that Dan Brown does not use gender inclusive language here!

people are abandoning God, truth and common sense in order to take on board Brown's radical teachings. Saint Paul in his Epistle to the Romans speaks of those who suppress the truth in unrighteousness. Of such people he says, "they are without excuse, because, although they knew God, they did not glorify *Him* as God, nor were thankful, but became futile in their thoughts, and their foolish hearts were darkened. Professing to be wise, they became fools … who exchanged the truth of God for the lie, and worshiped and served the creature rather than the Creator, who is blessed forever. Amen."[5] And this is precisely what Dan Brown is calling all of humankind to do: He is calling them to worship "the divine order of nature" in place of the Creator of Nature; to worship the creature, instead of the Creator. It is a return to pagan pantheism where Mother Earth — the goddess — is appointed as the master of creation, and where all is god and god is all. "My hope for *The Da Vinci Code*," says Brown on his website, "was that in addition to entertaining people that it might serve as an open door for readers to begin their own explorations and rekindle their interest in topics of faith."[6] But as Dr. Michael Green points out, Brown has "certainly has done that, and on an almost unparalleled scale. But the faith he is encouraging people into is a pick'n'mix of mysticism, with no transcendent deity, but with ancient goddess worship, Gnosticism and sexual permissiveness. It is a faith that sees this world as all there is, so we had better make the most of it."[7] But we believe in the Almighty God, the Maker of Heaven and Earth, the Father of our Savior and Redeemer Jesus Christ. He is the only living God; and the only true Lover of Mankind.

So dear reader, I ask you to be on your guard against those, who, like Dan Brown, come to you as wolves dressed in sheep's clothing. And I encourage you to not to be ignorant concerning your faith in your God, in His Church, and in His words of life and truth contained in the Holy Bible. For it is those who are ignorant who are easily deceived; and only those who are ready for battle who will emerge victorious. And

---

[5] Rom. 1:20–25.

[6] Brown, www.danbrown.com/novels/davinci_code/faqs.html.

[7] Green, *The Books the Church Suppressed*, 180–1.

finally, I leave you with the following words in the Coptic language from the Holy Midnight Psalmody of the Coptic Orthodox Church:

Ⲙⲁⲣⲉϥⲧⲱⲛϥ ⲛ̀ϫⲉ Ⲫ̀ⲛⲟⲩϯ ⲙⲁⲣⲟⲩϫⲱⲣ
ⲉ̀ⲃⲟⲗ ⲛ̀ϫⲉ ⲛⲉϥϫⲁϫⲓ ⲧⲏⲣⲟⲩ:
ⲙⲁⲣⲟⲩⲫⲱⲧ ⲉ̀ⲃⲟⲗ ϧⲁⲧ̀ϩⲏ
ⲙ̀ⲡⲉϥϩⲟ ⲛ̀ϫⲉ ⲟⲩⲟⲛ ⲛⲓⲃⲉⲛ
ⲉⲑⲙⲟⲥϯ ⲙ̀ⲡⲉϥⲣⲁⲛ ⲉⲑⲟⲩⲁⲃ:
Ⲇⲟⲝⲁⲥⲓ ⲫⲓⲗⲁⲛⲑ̀ⲣⲱⲡⲉ.

Let God arise;
let all His Enemies be scattered;
let all them that hate His Holy name
flee from before His face.
Glory be to You, O Lover of Mankind![8]

[8] Coptic excerpt (and its English translation) from the beginning of the Holy Midnight Psalmody, chanted daily at 4 AM in all Coptic monasteries.

Select Bibliography

AFP, "Stars Shrug Off 'Da Vinci Code' Reviews," Australian Broadcasting Corporation, 18 May, 2006. Accessed at www.abc.net.au/news/newsitems/200605/ s1641213.htm.

Alexander, V. "The Da Vinci Code," *FilmsInReview.com*, no date. Accessed at http://filmsinreview.com/.

Allen, J. L. *Opus Dei: An Objective Look Behind the Myths and Reality of the Most Controversial Force in the Catholic Church* (New York: Doubleday, 2005).

A Lion Handbook: The World's Religions, 1982 (Oxford: Lion Publishing, 1996).

Ansen, D. "A Disappointing 'Da Vinci Code,'" *Newsweek*, 18 May, 2006. Accessed at www.msnbc.msn.com/id/12853397/site/newsweek/page/2/.

Arendt, P. "The Da Vinci Code (2006)," *BBC*, 19 May, 2006. Accessed at www.bbc.co.uk/films/2006/05/18/the_da_vinci_code_2006 _review.shtml.

Athanasius, Saint. *St. Athanasius on the Incarnation: With an Introduction by C. S. Lewis*, 1944 (New York: St. Vladimir's Seminary Press, 2002).

_____. *On the Incarnation*, in *Nicene & Post-Nicene Fathers: Second Series* (*NPNF*), vol. 4.

_____. *Four Discourses Against the Arians: Discourse III* in *NPNF: Second Series*, 4.

_____. *Letter XXXIX (For 367.), NPNF*, 4.

_____. *Statement of Faith, NPNF: Second Series*, 4.

Athenagoras. *A Plea for the Christians*, in *Ante-Nicene Fathers* (*ANF*), vol. 2.

Baigent, M., Leigh, R., and Lincoln, H. *Holy Blood, Holy Grail*, 1982 (New York: Dell Publishing, 1983).

Barlowe, B. "Da Vinci Code: The Movie," *Leadership University*, no date. Accessed at www.leaderu.com/focus/davincicode.html.

BBC, "Brown Vindicated by Code Ruling," 7 April, 2006. Accessed at http://news.bbc.co.uk/2/hi/entertainment/4829736.stm.

_____. "Court Rejects Da Vinci Copy Claim," 7 April, 2006. Accessed at http://news.bbc.co.uk/2/hi/entertainment/4886234.stm.

_____. "Da Vinci Case Goes Back to Court," 9 August, 2006. Accessed at http://news.bbc.co.uk/2/hi/entertainment/4776657.stm.

Bell, J. "The Da Vinci Code," *Las Vegas Weekly*, 18 May, 2006. Accessed at www.lasvegasweekly.com/2006/05/18/davincicode.html.

Berardinelli, J. "The Da Vinci Code," *ReelViews*, no date. Accessed at http://movie-reviews.colossus.net/movies/d/davinci_code.html.

Bernard, J. "It didn't Work For Me: Howard's 'Da Vinci' is Paint-By-Numbers," *New York Daily News*, 18 May, 2006. Accessed at www.nydailynews.com/entertainment/movies/moviereviews/story/418787p-353581c.html.

Bettenson. H. (trans., ed.). *The Early Christian Fathers: A Selection from the Writings of the Fathers from St. Clement of Rome to St. Athanasius* (London: Oxford University Press, 1956).

Biancolli, A. "It's Just Like the Book, Without Any of the Interesting Parts," *Houston Chronicle*, 19 May, 2006. Accessed at www.chron.com/disp/story.mpl/ent/ movies/reviews/3835032.html.

Bodmer Papyrus II: *P66*, Gospel of John: Chapter 14–21 (Geneva: Bibliotheca Bodmeriana, 1961).

Bodmer Papyrus XVII: *P74*, The Acts of the Apostles: The Epistles of James, Peter, John, and Jude (Geneva: Bibliotheca Bodmeriana, 1962).

Bodmer Papyrus XIV–XV: *P75*, The Gospels of Luke and John: Book I: Luke Chapter 3–24 (Geneva: Bibliotheca Bodmeriana, 1961).

Bodmer Papyrus XIV–XV: *P75*, The Gospels of Luke and John: Book II: Chapter 1–15 (Geneva: Bibliotheca Bodmeriana, 1961).

Bonewits, I. *Neopagan Polytheology 101 (Version 5.6.5)*, 1974, 2005. Accessed at www.neopagan.net/NeopagansBelieve.html.

Boucher, "Does The Da Vinci Code Crack Leonardo?" *New York Times*, 3 August, 2003. Accessed at www.nytimes.com.

Brown, D. *Angels and Demons* (New York: Pocket Books, 2000).

_____. *Deception Point* (New York: Pocket Books, 2001).

_____. *Digital Fortress*, 1998 (New York: Saint Martin's Paperbacks, 2004).

_____. *The Da Vinci Code* (New York: Doubleday, 2003).

Channel4, "The Sacred Feminine: Father Sun, Mother Earth," no date. Accessed at www.channel4.com/culture/microsites/D/da_vinci_decoded/sacred.html.

Clement of Alexandria. *The Instructor*, *ANF*, 2.

_____. *Fragment XII.8*, *ANF*, 2.

Constitutions of the Holy Apostles, *ANF*, 7.

Corliss, R. "The Da Vinci Code Mystery Revealed!" *TIME Magazine*, 16 May, 2006. Accessed at http://time.blogs.com/movies/2006/05/the_ da_vinci_ co. html.

Cyprian, Saint. *Epistle LXXIII*, *ANF*, 5.

_____. *Epistle LXXV*, *ANF*, 5.

_____. *Epistle LXI*, *ANF*, 5.

_____. *Treatise X: On Jealousy and Envy*, *ANF*, 5.

_____. *Treatise XII: Second Book: Testimonies*, *ANF*, 5.

Dafoe, S. A. "Templar Myths: The Baphomet Mythos," *Templar History Magazine*, no date. Accessed at www.templarhistory.com/baphomet. html.

Da Vinci Code Deception, The. DVD, written by Joseph Meier, Grizzly Adams Productions, USA, no date.

Davis, L. D. *The First Seven Ecumenical Councils (325–787): Their History and Theology*, 1983 (Minnesota: Michael Glazier/The Liturgical Press, 1990).

Debraine, L. "Bestseller The Da Vinci Code is Based on a Deception," *Le Temps*, 15 March, 2004. Accessed at www.letemps.ch, http://priory-of-sion.com/psp/id80.html.

D'Emilio, F. "Opus Dei Asks for 'Da Vinci' Disclaimer," April 17, 2006. Accessed at www.cultofdanbrown.com/index.php/site/opus_dei_asks_for_da_vinci_ disclaimer/.

Douglas, J. D. (ed.). *The New International Dictionary of the Christian Church: Revised Edition*, 1974 (Zondervan Publishing House: Michigan, 1978).

Edersheim, A. *The Temple: Its Ministry and Services as They Were at the Time of Jesus Christ*, 1874 (Michigan: Angus Hudson and Kregel Publications, 1997).

Elliot, T. *The Christianity of Constantine the Great* (Bronx: University of Scranton Press, 1996).

Encyclopedia of the Early Church: 2 vols, A. Walford (trans.) (Oxford University Press: New York, 1992).

Etchegoin, M. F. "An Enquiry into the Sources of The Da Vinci Code," *Le Nouvel Observateur*, 9 September, 2004. Accessed at www. nouvelobs.com/articles/p2079/a248944.html.

Eusebius of Caesarea, *The Life of Constantine*, IV.36-7, *NPNF: Second Series*, 1.

Euteneuer, T. J. “The Da Vinci Mess — Part I: Sanitizing Satanism,” *Spirit & Life: Human Life International e-Newsletter*, 10 March, 2006. Accessed at http://spirit-and-life.blogspot.com/2006_04_23_spirit-and-life_archive. html.

_____. “The Da Vinci Mess — Final Edition: Leonardo’s Revenge,” *Spirit & Life: Human Life International e-Newsletter*, 19 May, 2006. Accessed at http://hli.org/sl_2006-05-19.html.

Ferguson, E. (ed.). *Encyclopedia of Early Christianity: Second Edition*, 1997 (New York and London: Garland Publishing, 1999).

Freedman, D. N. (ed.). *The Leningrad Codex: A Facsimile Edition* (Michigan: William B. Eerdmans Publishing Company and Leiden: Brill Academic Publishers, 1998).

Geisler, N. and Nix, W. *A General Introduction to the Bible: Revised and Expanded* (Chicago: Moody Press, 1986).

Gombrich, E. H. “Papers Given on the Occasion of the Dedication of the Last Supper (after Leonardo),” *Magdalen College Occassional Paper*, Magdalen College, Oxford, 10 March, 1993. Accessed from The Gombrich Archive at www.gombrich.co.uk/showdoc.php?id=26.

Gregory Nazianzen, Saint. *4th Theological Oration (on the Son)* in *NPNF: Second Series*, 7.

_____. *3rd Theological Oration (on the Son)* in *NPNF: Second Series*, 7.

Green, M. *The Books the Church Suppressed: Fiction and Truth in The Da Vinci Code* (Oxford and Michigan: Monarch Books, 2005).

Ignatius, Saint. *Epistle to the Ephesians*, *ANF*, 1.

_____. *Epistle to the Ephesians*, in Bettenson, H. (ed.), *The Early Christian Fathers: A Selection from the Writings of the Fathers from St. Clement of Rome to St. Athanasius* (London: Oxford University Press, 1956).

Irenaeus, Saint. *Against Heresies*, *ANF*, 1.

_____. *Proof of the Apostolic Preaching*, translated by Joseph P. Smith in *Ancient Christian Writers*: vol. 16 (New York: Paulist Press, no date).

Jones, A. "Case Study: The European Witch-Hunts, c. 1450–1750 and Witch- Hunts Today," no date. Accessed at www.gendercide.org/case_ witchhunts.html.

Justin Martyr, Saint. *Dialogue with Trypho*, *ANF*, 1.

Holy Psalmody, The. (NY: Saint Mary and Saint Antonios Coptic Orthodox Church, no date).

Kelley, P. H. *Biblical Hebrew: An Introductory Grammar* (Michigan: Eerdmans Publishing, 1992).

Kelly, J. N. D. *Early Christian Creeds: Third Edition*, 1950 (Essex: Longman, 1972).

_____. *Early Christian Doctrines: Fifth Edition*, 1958 (London: A & C Black, 1977).

Kenyon, F. G. *The Chester Beatty Biblical Papyri: Descriptions and Texts of Twelve Manuscripts on Papyrus on the Greek Bible: The Gospels and Acts* (London: Emery Walker, 1933).

_____. *The Chester Beatty Biblical Papyri: Descriptions and Texts of Twelve Manuscripts on Papyrus on the Greek Bible: Pauline Epistles* (London: Emery Walker, 1936).

_____. *The Chester Beatty Biblical Papyri: Descriptions and Texts of Twelve Manuscripts on Papyrus on the Greek Bible: Pauline Epistles and Revelation* (London: Emery Walker, 1934).

Lactantius. *The Divine Institutes*, *ANF*, 7.

Lane, A. "Heaven Can Wait: The Da Vinci Code," *New Yorker*, 22 May, 2006. Accessed at www.newyorker.com/critics/cinema/articles/060529 crci_ cinema.

Liungman, C. G. *Symbols '98 Encyclopedia*. Accessed from *Symbols.com: Online Encyclopedia of Western Signs and Ideograms* at www.symbols.com.

Malaty, T. Y. *A Panoramic View of Patristics in the First Six Centuries: With an Overview of Selected Coptic Orthodox Fathers and Authors of the Middle Ages* (Alexandria: Saint George's Coptic Orthodox Church, 2005).

Melito of Sardis, Bishop. *On Faith*, *ANF*, 8.

Miller, L. "The Last Word: The Da Vinci Con," *New York Times*, 22 February, 2004. Accessed at www.cesnur.org/2004/davinci_ nyt.htm.

_____. "The Da Vinci Crock," *Salon Magazine*, 29 December, 2004, Accessed at http://dir.salon.com/story/books/feature/2004/12/29/da_vinci_code/index1. html.

Mariampolski, R. "Secrets Hidden in Plain View: Dan Brown Delivers the Most Exciting Novel of the Season," no date. Accessed at www.bordersstores.com/features/feature.jsp?file=browndan.

Maslin, J. "Spinning a Thriller from the Louvre," *New York Times*, March 17, 2003. Accessed at www.nytimes.com.

Miesel, S. "Dismantling The Da Vinci Code," *Crisis Magazine*, September 1, 2003. Accessed at www.crisismagazine.com/september2003/feature1.htm.

Methodius. *The Banquet of the Ten Virgins*, *ANF*, 6.

Metzger, B. *The Canon of the New Testament: Its Origin, Development, and Significance* (Oxford: Clarendon Press, 1987).

Metzger, B. M. and Ehrman, B. D. *The Text of the New Testament: Its Transmission, Corruption, and Restoration: Fourth Edition* (Oxford and New York: Oxford University Press, 2005).

Molloy, M. E. *Champion of Truth: The Life of Saint Athanasius* (New York: Society of Saint Paul, 2003).

Morris, E. "Explosive New Thriller Explores Secrets of the Church," no date. Accessed at www.bookpage.com/0304bp/dan_brown.html.

Niederauer, G.H. "How Dark the Con of Man: Some Responses to The Da Vinci Code (The Novel and Soon the Film)," no date. Accessed at www.jesusdecoded.com/truthbetold1.php?page=100.

Olson, C. "Cracking Up The Da Vinci Code: Bad writing. Bad history. Bad theology. Did I Mention it Was Bad?" *Envoy Magazine*, 27 August, 2003. Accessed at www.envoymagazine.com/envoyencore/Detail.asp? BlogID=1124.

Pagels, E. *The Gnostic Gospels*, 1979 (New York: Vintage Books, 1989).

Pais, M. "Fast-Paised Review 'The Da Vinci Code': And You Thought Dan Brown's Bestseller Couldn't Get Any Bigger," *Chicago Tribune*, no date. Accessed at metromix.chicagotribune.com/movies/mmx-060519-movies-review-code -pais,0,3937053.story.

Perdue, L. *Daughter of God* (New York: Forge Books, 2000).

_____. *The Da Vinci Legacy*, 1983 (New York: TOR, 2004).

Phillips, J. *Exploring the World of the Jew*, 1981 (New Jersey: Loizeaux Brothers, 1993).

Phillips, M. "Movie Review: The Da Vinci Code," Chicago Tribune, no date. Accessed at http://metromix.chicagotribune.com/movies/mmx-060519-movies-review-code,0,931464.story.

Picknett, L. and Prince, C. *1997, The Templar Revelation: Secret Guardians of the True Identity of Christ* (Great Britain: Corgi Books, 1998).

Pope Shenouda III, His Holiness. *The Divinity of Christ* (London: COPA, 1989).

Puig, C. "For 'Da Vinci' Suspense, Read the Book," *USA Today*, 18 May, 2006. Accessed at www.usatoday.com/life/movies/reviews/2006-05-17-davinci - review_ x.html.

Reuters. "Boycott 'Da Vinci Code' Film: Top Vatican Official," April 30, 2006. Accessed at www.cultofdanbrown.com/index.php/site/boycott_da_ vinci_ code_film_ top _vatican _ official/.

Roberts, A. and Donaldson, J. (eds). *Ante-Nicene Fathers* (Massachusetts: Hendrickson Publishers, 1994.

Scott, A. O. "A 'Da Vinci Code' That Takes Longer to Watch Than Read," *New York Times*, 17 May, 2006. Accessed at http://movies2.nytimes.com/ 2006/05/17/ movies/17cnd-code.html.

Schaff, P. and Wace, H. (eds). *Nicene & Post-Nicene Fathers: Second Series* (Massachusetts: Hendrickson Publishers, 1995).

Severus Ibn al-Muqaffa'. *History of the Patriarchs of the Egyptian Church, Known as the History of the Holy Church.* Aziz Suryal Atiya, Yassa Abd al-Masih, and O.H.E.Khs.-Burmester (trans.) (Cairo, 1948).

Seattle Pacific University Magazine, "Decoding The Da Vinci Code: The Challenge of Historic Christianity to Post-Modern Fantasy," Summer 2005, Volume 28, Number 2. Accessed at www.spu.edu/depts/uc/response /summer2k5/ features/davincicode.asp.

Shea, M. and Sri, E. *The Da Vinci Deception: 100 Questions About the Facts and Fiction of The Da Vinci Code* (West Chester: Ascension Press, 2006).

Smith, P. "Da Vinci Code: Creating a New Age Version of Christianity?" no date. Accessed at http://priory-of-sion.com/dvc/newage.html.

_____. "Michael Baigent Profile and His Book The Jesus Papers," no date, Accessed at http://priory-of-sion.com/posd/baigent.html.

Starbird, M. *Goddess in the Gospels: Reclaiming the Sacred Feminine* (Rochester Vt.: Bear, 1998).

_____. *The Woman with the Alabaster Jar: Mary Magdalen and the Holy Grail* (Rochester Vt.: Bear, 1993).

Steinberg, L. *Leonardo's Incessant Last Supper* (New York: Zone Books, 2001).

Stevenson, J. (ed.). *Creeds, Councils, and Controversies: Documents Illustrative of the History of the Church A.D. 337–461*, 1966 (London: SPCK, 1973).

Tertullian. *De Fuga In Persecutione, ANF*, 4.

_____. *On Baptism, ANF*, 3.

_____. *Prescription Against Heretics, ANF*, 3.

_____. *On Repentance: Ch. VII, ANF*, 3.

Theophilus, Saint. *Theophilus to Autolycus, ANF*, 2.

The Three Coptic Divine Liturgies: Diocese of Sydney and Affiliated Regions: Study Version (Sydney: St. Mary and St. Mina's Coptic Orthodox College, 2002).

Wace, H. and Piercy, W. C. *A Dictionary of Christian Biography* (Massachusetts: Hendrickson Publishers, 1994).

Ward, B. *The Sayings of the Desert Fathers: The Alphabetical Collection*, 1975 (Michigan: Cisterican Publications, 1984).

_____ (trans.). *The Wisdom of the Desert Fathers*, 1975 (Oxford: SLG Press, 1986).

Waxman, S. "Da Vinci Code: The Mystery of the Missing Screenings," *New York Times*, 16 May, 2006. Accessed at www.nytimes.com/2006/05/16/movies/16code.

Wilkinson, P. *Illustrated Dictionary of Religions: Figures, Fetivals, and Beliefs of the World's Religions* (London: Dorling Kindersley Publishing, 1999).

Young, F. *From Nicaea to Chalcedon* (London: SCM Press, 1983).

_____. *The Making of the Creeds* (London: SCM Press, and Philadelphia: Trinity Press International, 1991).

About the Author

His Eminence Metropolitan Bishoy is one of the foremost theologians in present-day Christendom. Since his ordination as bishop by His Holiness Pope Shenouda III in the Holy Coptic Orthodox Church in 1972, His Eminence has been Bishop of the Diocese of Damiette, Kafr el-Sheikh, and Barrary, as well as the Abbot of the Monastery of Saint Demiana and the Forty Virgins for nuns; all located in Egypt. In 1985, His Eminence was elected as the General Secretary of the Holy Synod of the Coptic Orthodox Church, and in 1990 he was ordained and elevated to the rank of Metropolitan. His Eminence is a member of the Executive Committee and the Standing Committee of Faith and Order in the World Council of Churches; he is co-chairman of all theological dialogues between the Oriental Orthodox family of churches and other denominations; and he lectures in dogmatic and comparative Theology, and ecumenism at fifteen seminaries and theological colleges throughout Egypt, Australia, England, and Germany. His Eminence Metropolitan Bishoy resides in Egypt.